MY LIFE
AS A ROSE-BREASTED
GROSBEAK

My Life as a Rose-Breasted Grosbeak

STUART TRUEMAN

Illustrated by the Author

McClelland and Stewart Limited
Toronto

ACKNOWLEDGEMENTS

Women Are Crazy About Money, Husbands Tell the Worst Stories, It's Easy to Train Your Memory, Family Travel Can Be Fun, Women Leave Me Speechless, You're Darn Tootin', Carry Me Back to Old Hypochondria, Everything's Up to Date in Dear Old Blighty, I'm All Wrapped Up for Christmas, Yule Greetings Yule Never Get, The Christmas Ties That Bind, Thanks for the Lovely Christmas Present, and Smile, Darn You, Kiddies — You Too, Rover, originally appeared in *Weekend Magazine*.

My Life as a Rose-Breasted Grosbeak originally appeared in *Colliers*.

How to Train for Your Vacation, The Importance of Being Somebody, and How to Show Your Appreciation in a Zestful, Palate-Tingling Way originally appeared in *Macleans Magazine*.

Dog People Are Peculiar, and Some Other Time, Pal! originally appeared in *Atlantic Advocate*.

Could I See a Good Murder? originally appeared in *Star Weekly*.

How I Missed the Flu, and Hark, Hark, the Song of the Lark originally appeared in *Saturday Evening Post*.

Two Cheese Sandwiches, Our Shiftless Birds, and A Good Rest at Home originally appeared in *Saturday Night*.

The Case of the Disappearing Den originally appeared in *Canadian Homes*.

How I Kept My Resolutions, It's Not True What They Say About Women Back-Seat Drivers, How the Lawn-Chair Business Folded Up, Maneuvers in the Barber Shop, and How to Sell Tickets originally appeared in *Maritime Merchant*.

The Canadian Publishers
McClelland and Stewart Limited
25 Hollinger Road, Toronto 374

Printed and bound in Canada by
The Alger Press Limited

CONTENTS

Birds, Beasts
and
the Common
Man

Dog People
are Peculiar

What makes pedigreed dog owners so envious? Look at my neighbor Herb Frobisher. He's taking his Labrador retriever to one of the newfangled Obedience Schools instead of letting me help train him. Why? Just because he can't bear to think I know more about dogs than he does.

Goodness knows I showed Herb a lot about his last pet, an Irish setter.

"It says right here in my dog behavior book," I told him, "the way to housebreak a pup is to get up earlier than he does, and hurry him outdoors."

Herb got up the next morning at 7. Too late. The pup was awake.

On the second morning Herb dashed into the kitchen at 6, and rushed the drowsy dog out.

"That was a great tip," he told me gratefully. "A couple of mornings more and we'll be all trained."

But when Herb sprinted into the kitchen at 6 the following morning, the pup was sitting up watching. It knew what time to expect him. Too late.

So Herb set the alarm for 5.30, which proved to be fine — for two days.

Then he set it for 5, and 4.30, and 4.

Puzzled neighbors soon heard about Herb's forays out with the pup in the wee sma' hours. Some said he must be partying every night, and it was a shame to come home so late and wake up the little dog and make him walk.

Poor Herb found he had to go to bed by 9 P.M. to get up at 3.30.

When he and his wife went out Saturday night to visit friends, Herb had no sooner settled in a chair and been handed a drink when he began to snore in their faces.

If this wasn't embarrassing enough for Herb, it was worse to wake up a few moments later and hear the hostess saying in a glaring whisper: "DON'T ... GIVE ... HIM ... ANY ... MORE."

I'll say for Herb he was impartial. He didn't sleep only at friends' homes: He dozed off at office conferences, at lunch with customers, at the barber shop, even in the dentist's chair. This drew some caustic comment from his boss, Colonel Barkville, but also won approving remarks from the dentist on Herb's new nonchalance while getting his jaw frozen. He likened it admiringly to Churchill's ability to snatch a few winks at any time during World War II. Nevertheless the rumor gained widespread credence that Herb couldn't be persuaded to get off the stuff, whatever it was, night or day.

There was one nice consolation for Herb, though, as I pointed out to cheer him up. You see, as a surprise I had taught the pup to bring him his morning newspaper from the railway stationmaster. After all, what's a dog for if he can't fetch something useful? The only trouble was, the second morning Herb opened the front door to find twenty-nine rolled-up newspapers on his doorstep! That smart dog was so eager to please that he hadn't waited to get the right one from the stationmaster.

"You're lucky to be up so early," I told Herb. "You've got time to take them all back to the stationmaster, or deliver them around if you don't like to face him, ha, ha!"

Herb didn't laugh. He didn't even thank me for taking the trouble. That's when I began to suspect that dog people are a self-centered lot. But I refused to let it get me down.

In fact, it was the very next day that I offered to show Herb how to bring out the natural tracking and retrieving instincts of his Irish setter.

"Play hide-and-go-seek!" I urged. "My book says it keeps a sporting dog on his toes. See — I'll hold him; you go hide and holler 'Come!'"

Herb ran down to the end of his driveway and crouched behind a lilac bush.

"Come!" he shouted.

The dog didn't pay any attention. He was looking up at

a redwing blackbird in a tree. Besides, he knew I had treats in my pocket.

"Come!" yelled Herb again, motionless.

It was just then that Colonel Barkville and his wife strolled along. They saw Herb squatting in the shrubbery. Colonel Barkville walked past staring. His wife looked the other way.

"How do you do," Colonel Barkville said coldly.

Naturally Herb couldn't answer; the dog might hear him. Nor could he move; the dog might see him. All he could do was smile and wiggle his eyebrows at the Colonel.

It didn't seem to have the right effect. Colonel Barkville, even when far up the sidewalk, was still frowning backward over his shoulder. He seemed baffled, I don't know why. Anyone could surely see Herb was playing hide-and-go-seek with a dog.

The incident seemed to discourage Herb, but it didn't discourage me. In fact, when his pup began to display an alarming new tendency a few days later — an urge to chase every car going by — I had the answer right away.

"Teach him a lesson!" I advised. "Break the habit at the outset! Punish him at the very moment — that's what my book says — so he'll know what it's for."

Quickly I persuaded Herb to lie down on the back floor of his car, with the door open and a rolled-up magazine in his hand, while I drove the car slowly past the end of his driveway.

For some reason, the dog didn't show any interest. He didn't want to chase Herb's car. Every time the car crept by, with Herb's motionless bald head protruding through the open doorway and the magazine held ready, the dog either scratched his ear or stared up in the tree for birds.

The dog just looked as if, from his standpoint, this was the way his master always came home.

Colonel Barkville evidently thought the same thing. He kept staring from a short distance up the sidewalk. I don't think it helped very much that I, as a friend driving his car, couldn't appear to find the driveway and kept passing it.

That was several weeks ago. I haven't seen much of Herb

since — not since his unexpected early retirement from the firm.

His Irish setter is with Herb's sister now up country, where there are lots of birds in the trees and no traffic, and Herb has bought this new Labrador. I have a dandy notion out of my dog book to tell Herb — you give a pup an old shoe for his very own, and then he won't bother your other shoes!

I've already tried it on Bill Bartley next door, who has a German shepherd pup, but I don't think Bill went about it the right way. When he gave the pup an old shoe, it got the idea somehow that shoes were for chewing. Bill came home one night and found all his six pairs of good shoes in tatters.

I'd like to tell Herb the good news about how to save his shoes but, as I said, he seems to be avoiding me. He realizes I know more about dogs than he does, and he has had all of it he can take.

My Life
as a Rose-Breasted
Grosbeak

Bird lovers make me nervous. They twitter; they flutter; in flights of fancy they soar completely out of this world to one of their own, where people and birds talk freely and understand every word.

If you've ever in all innocence gone to lunch with an otherwise rational businessman and had to wait while he trilled at the restaurant's canary, trying to make it trill back at him, you'll know what I mean. It's embarrassing enough without your tycoon cocking his head coyly this way and that to convince the canary he's a bird too. The canary never says a word; it thinks he's crazy.

The worst of it is, you can't tell beforehand who may be a secret bird lover masquerading as a normal person. There's Mr. Plumpton — a level-headed power magnate if ever I saw one. He loves to level things. His eyes gleam impatiently when he sees a contented village he can raze to build a hydro-electric plant. He likes to drive the bulldozer that knocks down the houses, preferably before the people get out. In other words, he gives every appearance of being a sane and progressive citizen.

When he summons me to draw up an estimate on hauling away the rubble of East Shadydale, which he demolished last week to give his new bulldozer a workout, I expect to hear talk about nothing but kilowatts and power potential.

I call at his mansion and am shown into the palatial living room. The door from the veranda bursts open. It is Mr. Plumpton. He is feverishly excited. "She's back! She's back!" he cries. Has his wife returned to him? No; something far more important than that. He is positive he has seen the same chickadee that perched on the veranda railing last summer. He's been saying to it, "Beepety-bee-bee-bee-bee." The chickadee is fascinated, and little wonder. It thinks he is an automobile horn.

When we get into my car to drive to East Shadydale, he snatches up something from the floor of the car. "Look what I've found!" he says in amazement. For a moment I think it's a ten-dollar bill. It turns out to be a feather — "a beautiful specimen of the purple-crested lourie's plumage." He can't figure out how it got into the car. I could tell him it came out of our feather duster, but I don't. Let him puzzle over it. It may keep him quiet.

He is not, however, quiet long. As we approach an intersection he bellows: "Look out — on your *left!*"

I swerve to the right and jam on the brakes.

"What was it?" I quaver. "I can't see anything."

"It's a yellow-billed cuckoo," he whispers. "On the lower branch of the apple tree. First one I've seen all season."

I can see the tree but I can't see the bird, nor do I want to.

"I've been watching for a white-breasted nuthatch," Mr. Plumpton goes on. "Did you know that the white-breasted nuthatch spends much of its life upside down?" The white-breasted nuthatch, I reflect, isn't the only one.

Now, thank goodness, we've arrived at East Shadydale — or what's left of it. Mr. Plumpton flits around like a hummingbird, examining the wreckage with satisfaction.

Suddenly he grasps my arm. "Sh-h-h-h!" He leads me back toward the car. "Never mind. It can't be started now. The job will have to wait — four weeks, maybe five. Did you see what I saw?"

"What?"

"A pair of blue-headed vireos! They've built a nest in the debris. It has three teeny-weeny eggs in it." He is speaking in hushed tones. "You can't run trucks in here. The daddy and mummy would fly away and never come back."

As we start for home, I decide there is nothing for me to do now but give in. The birds have beaten me. I let him talk, and concur in everything he says. He points out a gray-cheeked thrush, and I exclaim over it. I obediently admire, in turn, a red-bellied sapsucker, an olive-sided fly-catcher and a blue-gray gnatcatcher.

Meanwhile he teaches me to distinguish bird notes. "Cheep, cheep!" he is saying as we pull into a service station for gas. "Cheep, cheep!" I repeat. The garage man listens, speechless, as Mr. Plumpton admonishes, "Higher — higher! *Cheep, cheep, cheep!* You'll never attract a mate singing like that from a treetop!" The man doesn't know it, but he is waiting for a couple of rose-breasted grosbeaks to decide how much gas they want. He fills up the tank anyway.

We are mourning doves when we start back for Mr. Plumpton's house, and when we're almost there, Mr. Plumpton whoops, "My! Just look at those beautiful legs!"

I keep my eyes on the road and don't even glance. I know it's a stilt-legged crane or a red-limbed goochbill. A moment later, when it's too late to look, he ponders aloud, "She's a secretary downtown somewhere — Shirley, I think her name is."

As I said, bird watchers drive me crazy.

Our Shiftless Birds

Something will have to be done about the birds in this country. They are not keeping up with birds in other countries. Too much time is being spent in chattering on the telephone wires while birds elsewhere are doing things worth while.

Two recent news dispatches from abroad were significant to anyone who has noticed the decline of pioneering spirit among modern Canadian birds.

One item, from Ealing, London — just an obscure paragraph, as the editor entirely missed its importance — told of "a bird that looked like an owl" power-diving down and snatching the spectacles off the nose of a Mr. C. J. Orme. A moment later a bird swooped on a Mr. William Kysow and away went his spectacles too.

Naturally the bird "looked like an owl," because it was an owl. Only owls wear spectacles, as Messrs. Orme and Kysow should know if they ever read the comic books.

If I remember, the owl also fancies a "mortarboard" hat, and carries a teacher's pointer to show people in advertisements where they can save money. Mr. Orme and Mr. Kysow should be thankful they were wearing unsuitable hats and were not just coming out of the choir loft.

This brings up the question of Canadian owls. Nature intended them to dress properly, but left it to their initiative to furnish themselves, just as humans are born without spectacles. Are they doing anything about it? Not that I have seen in the papers. They are sitting around on three branches, idly watching the girl owls go by, and looking slovenly and short-sighted as if they didn't care a hoot anyway.

It is easy to say, "Oh, well, the British government gives

15

away spectacles and the English owls knew they weren't depriving Mr. Orme and Mr. Kysow of anything." It does our own owls no favor to make excuses for them. They are not being considerate of us but just plain lazy.

The other dispatch, from the Australian News Service, told about "bower birds" which are so enterprising they paint the walls of their nests. It claimed they chew up wood to make a paint-paste, and wield a piece of bark in their bill as a brush. I remember this, although I have unfortunately mislaid the dispatch, because my house needed painting and I was thinking if I were a bower bird it would take quite a while to do one wall. It was obvious you needed the right shape of bill, and I dismissed the thought. Nevertheless it indicates Australian birds are not only ahead of our birds but also of many of us.

The Australian News people usually carry things too far, in my opinion, and spoil the credibility of the story. This account went on to allege that some bower birds paint with laundry bluing and one bird collected eighteen bags of it. How could one bird have a nest big enough to need eighteen bags of bluing? Are they going to tell us next this bird happens to be an apartment block owner? I would not be surprised.

Since reading these items I have tried, on behalf of the advancement of Canadian feathered folk, to teach a friendly blackbird the niceties of living. When I saw it on the windowsill, curiously watching me paint a chair, I just let the industrious example sink in. Before tip-toeing away I carefully opened the window, placing some bags of bluing within reach, and a copy of "The Apartment Beautiful" lying open at a double-page spread of the William Stanstead III residence on Long Island.

Things certainly happened.

When I returned, the bluing and the book were undisturbed but the silver cufflinks were gone off my dresser and I couldn't find my new fountain pen.

16

Hark, Hark,
the Song
of the Lark

"A blackbird at Croydon, heard at 5.01 A.M., appears to have been the earliest songbird out recently, according to reports from bird watchers at four hundred points who took a census of the 'dawn to dusk' chorus. Mr. Noble Rollin of the Bird Research Station at Glanton, Northumberland, reported a robin heard at 5.03 A.M., a song thrush at 5.07, a chaffinch at 5.51, a greenfinch at 5.54, a yellowhammer at 5.57." — English news item.

In my effort to win this record away from England for North America, I watched all last night from my boarding house window at 5506½ Columbus Ave. It was very interesting. My log says:

4.30 A.M. — The whole neighborhood is expecantly quiet. The only light is in Mrs. Schmatz' window across the alley; I can see her sitting up reading a book.

4.57 A.M. — Zero hour is near. No birds yet. Milkman is walking up the alley.

4.58 A.M. — A beautiful chirp — "Thweeet" — which must surely be a robin.

4.59 A.M. — The trill seems to be coming from the alley entrance, where I almost imagine I see a man's head peeking around. The milkman is walking back to investigate.

5.00 A.M. — My heart leaps when I hear the milkman say, "Well, well — you're an early bird," but the robin turns out to be Mr. Schmatz. He has worked very late and looks extremely drowsy. He whispers thickly, "Is the old magpie up yet?"

5.01 A.M. — The milkman cranes his neck, trying to see a nest which must be near Mrs. Schmatz' windowsill, and whispers back, "The old magpie's up."

I have marked down: "5.01 — One magpie." This gives me at least a tie with Mr. Noble Rollin.

5.02 A.M. — The milkman has helped Mr. Schmatz through the alley to his back door where, in the darkness, they seem to be chuckling over a joke. There is quite a clanking of milk bottles.

5.03 A.M. — Mr. Schmatz has told the milkman, "One swallow doesn't make a summer, you know." The milkman says, "That's right, but I shouldn't wait for another." I have marked down: "5.03 — One swallow; others expected." I am keeping pace with Mr. Noble Rollin.

5.04 A.M. — Addressing a bird I cannot see, Mr. Schmatz has commented, "You can't fly on one wing, you know." I just note this down tentatively as "Species vague; probably incapacitated." The milkman, a bird fancier himself, readily agrees with Mr. Schmatz' observation.

5.15 A.M. — Mr. Schmatz and the milkman have started to sing "We Are Feathered Friends in Our Nest," with frequent interruptions because each wants to sing tenor.

5.16 A.M. — As I was writing the above, something winged its way past my window from Mrs. Schmatz' direction and struck Mr. Schmatz. It may have been a yellowhammer, but I am not taking credit for it.

5.16½ A.M. — The back door has opened suddenly and Mr. Schmatz has gone in quickly, almost as if flying off his feet. I think they must be moving the furniture around. The racket is terrific. I might as well go to bed now, but I am not conceding victory to Mr. Noble Rollin. I am going to try again to break the record; perferably some day when I am visiting Glanton, Northumberland.

The
Frustrated
Male

How I Kept
My Resolutions

Well, how are you making out with your New Year's resolutions? There's no need to answer; I shouldn't have asked. Mine are all broken too, just like the Christmas toys; I'd just as soon not be reminded of them.

One of the interesting phenomena of our times is that everybody, but everybody, makes New Year's resolutions. There's something about making them that purifies the soul, raises the spirits, stimulates the imagination, expands the mind, unfolds sublime vistas of anticipation. They give you a wonderful lift, and they don't cost a cent.

When you see a man at a gala New Year's Eve ball wearing a pink paper hat with silver half-moons, teetering in the middle of the floor at 11.59 P.M. with his eyes shut tight and his lips working spasmodically, you may think he's on a trip, trying to figure out why his tongue has changed to flannel. But he's not. He's telling himself how good he's going to be next year.

It's easy to know what he's going to be good about. If he has a glass clenched in his hand and is taking quick gulps from it, with one eye squinting at the clock, he's promising he won't touch another drink for twelve months.

If he has one arm wrapped around a brunette, the other squeezing the life out of a blonde, he's vowing he'll never look at a woman again and will settle down and be a huge success in his business.

There's something about a New Year's resolution that always impels people to make the most of the few minutes left in the dying year.

I know this myself. I always resolve to stop smoking, which to a heavy smoker is life's greatest challenge. The

20

very thought of it makes me take out a cigarette and start puffing furiously. I want to get in all the smoking I can before the bells start clanging and horns blaring.

Then, for good measure, I throw in some stock resolutions which I have made so often at New Year's that I don't have to think them up fresh any more.

I resolve to be frank and forthright with everyone, to do setting-up exercises every morning without fail, to be calm and pleasant at all times no matter what the provocation, and keep careful watch on my weight.

It's strange what happens to my resolutions. I never break them. They just seem to break themselves.

For instance when I'm leaving the party at 4.30 A.M., portly Mrs. McDrinkle, who is convulsed with laughter as she tries to walk along the crack between the floor and the wall in the corridor, under the impression that the hallway has tipped over since she came in, collides with me and sends me flying down the front steps into a muddy slush puddle.

"Oh, dear me!" she shrieks happily. "I've pushed you into the wet — your leg's soaked! Aren't I the clumsy cow!"

"Not at all," I reply graciously. "It was my fault. No harm done."

This, I immediately realize, is the finish of my resolution about being frank and forthright. I've fallen into polite lying again. She *was* a clumsy cow. It *wasn't* my fault. And some harm *was* done; my pants will have to be dry-cleaned. I wish I had told her off, but it's too late now — she's disappeared into a taxi, laughing hilariously at how everybody seems to be bumping into her.

Naturally, when I finally get to bed, I don't wake up until the afternoon of New Year's Day. The happy thought occurs to me right away — I don't have to bother with the morning setting-up exercises; I've missed the very first morning of the year, so it's no use now. The resolution is smashed beyond repair.

And then the resolve about being calm and pleasant at all times — I really meant to observe that one. Emergencies would not ruffle me. The roof might fall down, the furnace blow up, someone come along and steal the veranda, and all the time I

21

would be nodding and smiling to everyone, speaking in well modulated tones.

Unfortunately on New Year's Day, while I'm waiting for something big like the roof to fall down, the dog runs off with my bedroom slippers. Now if there's something a man needs on that particular day, when his shoe laces stubbornly refuse to go into even the most studiously contrived loops and keep flying out of his fingers before he can knot them, it's his bedroom slippers. So I roar at the dog, and it's just as well he can't understand what I'm shouting. But my wife can. She points out I should have made a New Year's resolution about keeping calm. It's too late now to make it over again; it's shattered.

As far as the resolution about watching my weight is concerned, I discover on New Year's Day that I have failed completely to take into account the big dinner coming up in the evening. Of all the silly resolutions to make on New Year's Eve! So it's quite a relief to remember a moment later that I only promised to *watch* my weight, not to reduce it.

I am keeping this resolution very well, if you look at it that way. My weight has gone up nine pounds since New Year's, and I'm happy to report I'm watching it with the closest of interest.

Oh yes, and the resolution about not smoking. I don't know what I could have been thinking of to promise that. A fellow can't just stop smoking right in the middle of a party. He will just turn cranky and spoil everyone's fun. He should wait for a nice quiet Sunday, when there is nothing on his mind to worry him or excite him. So that is what I'm doing. I'm waiting for a nice quiet Sunday at home, but I'm not expecting to encounter one in the near future.

That's how I've kept my New Year's resolutions. Many people will probably consider them to be irreparably broken, but I don't consider them broken in the strictest sense of the word. I've kept them in perfect condition, as good as new, hardly used at all. So they should do just fine again next New Year's.

It's Easy
to Train
Your Memory!

One of the commonest failings of husbands, according to a recent survey, is forgetting their wedding anniversaries — "about 90 per cent of wives complained of this."

Apparently most wives didn't feel so bad about their birthdays being overlooked, generously putting this down to man's natural absent-mindedness. Some wives, out of consideration for their husbands, even stopped having them.

But wedding anniversaries were different. They expected a present.

The saddest part about this husbandly lapse, I think, is that it's so unnecessary. The failing can be very easily cured.

All you need is a simple system. Here, in the hope it may help others, is how I worked out mine:

First I suggested a mutual-aid pact to a friend, Herb Frobisher, whose wedding anniversary falls on the same day. He was enthusiastic.

"Swell!" said Herb. "Two heads are better than one — whoever thinks of the date first will remind the other fellow."

It was a great relief to both our heads to leave it to the other fellow.

I can't figure out why, but the next year we both forgot. Herb seemed a little put out with me because it was my idea. But how could anyone expect me to provide the idea and do all the remembering as well?

Then I hit on an inspiration: I made a note on my office date pad for the following year — not in spelled-out words, of course, so anyone else might know my private business, but just "WED. ANN."

"O.K., I'm banking on you," said Herb happily. "Be sure to phone me."

It worked, too! A year later, on the morning of my wedding anniversary, I saw the message immediately. In fact, I stared at it for some time. It was printed quite clearly — "WED. ANN." The only thing I couldn't understand was who "Ann" was — I knew several Anns — and what was I supposed to do with her next Wednesday. I knew, of course, that "WED. ANN." couldn't mean I was supposed to marry her.

I became worried. I thought the cryptic note might puzzle me forever.

At supper time my wife said: "Do you know what day this is?"

"No. What?"

"Oh — never mind. It isn't important."

Something about the way she said it brought a sharp twinge of memory. I'd heard that flat tone before — on our wedding anniversary last year! But once again I didn't have a present. Consequently, the day was ruined.

Next morning a wonderful idea struck me: I would make a note ahead on my desk pad so I wouldn't get caught next year! I carefully wrote down "WED. ANN." Then, like a flash, it came to me what yesterday's note had meant. So you can see it didn't puzzle me very long.

Naturally I erased "WED. ANN." then, so there wouldn't be any more confusion with Wednesday and Ann. I printed instead "WEDDING AN." — just to tip me off.

This seemed to mollify Herb Frobisher, who had called up sounding almost bad-tempered, as though I had missed seeing the note altogether.

"Don't forget, then," said Herb, perking up again. "I'll be looking for the old phone call!"

When the date rolled around a year later, sure enough there it was on the pad, plain as anything: "WEDDING AN." I studied it closely. It was my own printing, no doubt about that. Obviously I had made a note about a wedding; but whose? And why hadn't I written "A WEDDING"? What on earth had possessed me not only to reverse the words but also use bad grammar?

It was baffling. Even my wife couldn't help me. I phoned

and asked: "Do you know anyone getting married today?" and she said, "No."

That's how she caught me at supper time without a present again. I felt pretty peeved, as any busy husband will understand. "I had it marked on my pad," I insisted, "but you wouldn't tell me whose wedding it was." She couldn't see this. She wouldn't admit it. That's a peculiarity about wives. They won't face up to facts. They'd rather be martyrs.

At Herb Frobisher's house, things were worse. Poor Herb. When his wife said: "Do you know what day this is?" he replied offhand, "Haven't a notion."

"Think!" she said grimly.

"I can't imagine."

"Think *hard*. What was the happiest day in your life?"

Herb thought a moment. Then he brightened.

"The day I won the case of beer at the lodge raffle!"

By the time Herb arrived at my door, banging needlessly loud, with one side of his face crimson as if it had bumped into something, I had an infallible plan all worked out.

"It's a cinch!" I told him eagerly. "We'll let our *wives* remind us. They always remember the date — that's been the whole trouble. All we have to do is each keep a present hidden away until the girls say: 'Do you know what day this is?' That's our cue."

"Say, that's a stroke of genius!" Herb admitted with reluctant admiration, his tight-clenched mouth relaxing. "I'll get mine in the morning. Now we're orbiting!"

That was last year — now we're all set.

Each of us has lost only one present so far. Herb lost his through sheer stupidity. When his wife said, "Do you know what day this is?" he rushed upstairs and brought down the present and said, "How's this for remembering?" As his eyes lighted with anticipation, she opened the box of toiletries and cried: "Oh, isn't this sweet! Mother will be delighted — you've never been so thoughtful before." Herb just stared as she went on: "Don't forget — it's the 8.35 train you're supposed to meet."

Herb, you see, isn't very smart sometimes. Myself, I lost my present through simple bad luck. I put the boxed earrings on the top shelf of an upstairs closet, where I was sure no one ever dusted. When my wife found it while dusting the next morning, I couldn't let her in on our anniversary system and spoil everything.

"It's — it's for you," I blurted, "I mislaid it last Christmas The dog must have carried it away."

As the shelf is 6½ feet high, I sometimes wonder if she was really convinced.

Herb and I have each hidden away another present (back of our furnaces, where we know for sure no one will dust, as that's our job). And as we're getting near the anniversary date — I'm not exactly certain when it is — we're pretty excited.

All we hope now is that after all the trouble we've gone to, our wives won't fail to remember. That's our only worry. As Herb remarked yesterday, and I nodded in agreement: "If there's one thing I can't stand, it's to have somebody let you down."

Some
Other Time,
Pal!

With so much attention being given to drawing up uniform traffic signals these days, I'd like to suggest one that needs drawing up pretty badly.

It's a signal to inform my friend Sam McCool, standing on the street corner, that I can't pick him up — much as I would like to — because I'm not going as far as he's going.

This is a serious problem, believe me. I start out in the car for, say, the supermarket a mile away. There on the curb is my friend Sam, waiting for the bus to take him to town, five miles away. He's looking at me hopefully.

If I shake my head, tight-lipped, he may think I'm saying, "I wouldn't give *you* a lift."

If I smile ostentatiously as I shake my head, that's worse. He thinks I'm not only turning him down but gloating over him.

My wife suggested I should just nod and point ahead with one finger as I pass. Isn't that absurd? He can see which way I'm going — the same way he's going. Pointing is pointless; it just rubs it in.

Usually I follow one of two alternatives: (a) Pretend I'm looking somewhere else, which doesn't fool either of us; or (b) Slow down and open the door of the car to call out and explain to him. This is the worst choice yet. The moment I slow down, he perks up; when I open the door, he jumps in and stretches out with a grateful exclamation, leaving me nothing to do but drive him wherever he's going.

There is, of course, an alternative I haven't mentioned: I could clip him off the curb. But that would be only a temporary remedy. There would be someone else on the corner tomorrow. What I need is a signal.

27

Husbands
Tell
the Worst Stories

According to a London institute of human relations, the greatest cause of marital discord is monotony.

This, of course, is nonsense.

The greatest cause is the strange reluctance of husbands to let their wives help tell a story.

I've seen it often. Husbands are peculiar in this respect. They resent helpfulness. They are jealous of a woman's ability to get to the crux of the matter.

Like Herb Frobisher, regaling the neighborhood gang with his favorite anecdote about how he rushed from his summer cottage down to the shore to greet his brother-in-law.

"When I heard the outboard," Herb relates ebulliently, savoring the anticipation on everyone's face, "I shouted, 'Hurry, everybody, grab the picnic baskets, all aboard!' And then — "

"It was only a chain-saw across the river," Stella Frobisher interjects.

Sudden silence.

Herb gives Stella a slow, awful look.

"*Was* it only a chain-saw?" asks someone.

"Yes!" laughs Stella. "Wasn't that silly? Herb couldn't tell the difference."

Now, that is thoughtful of Stella; she has condensed the last five minutes of Herb's story into one brief sentence that explains everything. She has saved him the need of telling how he ran eagerly to the beach, a basket in one hand, waving at a dark speck that turned out to be a log snagged on a rock.

But is he grateful? That's the odd part of it. He has left the room. He's out in the kitchen glaring at the wall.

See what I mean? He knows she can tell a story better than he can.

"Herb!" calls out Stella's happy voice, oblivious of his behavior. "Tell them about the bear!"

Eyes lighting up, her husband troops back into the living room. He's always an optimist. He holds up his hands for quiet.

"It was our first night at the camp," he chuckles, "and we'd seen big animal tracks in the sand. Well, sir, I was about to put out the lights when I heard this low *growwwl*. I snatched up the shotgun, my hands trembling — "

"It was only the hammock," Stella announces.

Very slowly, Herb turns and stares at her.

"It *was* the hammock," she insists, laughing. "Don't you remember? The wind was blowing, and the hook-things made a growling sound. . . . *Herb!* Where are you going?"

He has stomped out again. That's the trouble with husbands; when they find how good their wives are at story telling, they can't take it.

Stella hurries after him. He has downed a quick glass of punch, and is holding his forehead.

"Please, Herb," she says, properly admonishing him, "don't act like a spoiled boy. Everyone is noticing it. Come back and join the fun."

"But you never let me finish a story!" he groans.

You have to admire Stella's restraint.

"All I said," she replies, "was that it was the hammock. And it was."

He couldn't deny it.

"Come on," she says brightly. "Tell them about the tape recorder; they'll get a big bang out of that!"

Herb, I may have indicated, is a bear for punishment. He starts grinning at the recollection.

"You won't interrupt me?"

"I never interrupt you," she says with earnestness. "It's just that you take so *long* to get to the point."

A moment later, eyes glistening, he begins:

"It had been raining all through my vacation at the camp, so I phoned the boss to see if I could take an extra day; he said no, things were too busy."

Quickly he glances aside at Stella, like a pitcher watching the runner on first. But — wonder of wonders — she is mum.

Encouraged, Herb continues:

"About 8 o'clock the last morning, I was startled out of my sleep by a loud knock on the door. I jumped from bed in my pajama bottoms — and out the window I could see an arm holding a tape recorder. I knew in an instant it was one of those canvassers with a talking sales-pitch. Well, sir, I breathed fire — "

"It was his boss," Stella says gleefully.

Herb looks dazed; he slowly heads for the kitchen.

To her bewilderment Stella finds him sitting limply on a stool, his head buried in his hands.

"You didn't give me a chance," the muffled voice moans, "to tell them how I shouted through the door to get the blazes off the veranda."

"And you didn't give *me* a chance," she retorts, "to say why he brought the tape recorder; so you could stay longer and do your dictation."

Stella, of course, is right. Herb *hasn't* been very considerate.

"Now come back," she orders, "or our friends will think you're acting so childish they'll never speak to you again."

Following her in, Herb pleads, *"You* tell a story, dear. There's something wrong with me tonight. Everything I tell seems to go wrong."

"All right!" says Stella blithely, speaking more to the party than to him. "I'll tell a story! This is one I didn't even tell Herb yet, because I knew he'd only get terribly upset."

Through glazed eyes Herb looks up at her.

"It was the morning Herb went into town to get the groceries," Stella starts off. "I heard over the radio about the three Dennessey gangsters escaping from the penitentiary only four miles away — "

"The *awful* ones?" cries Hilda McCool eagerly. "The ones who attack women wherever they go?"

30

"They were the ones," affirms Stella. "You saw their pictures in the papers. *Ugh!* That monster with the hairy bristle on his face!"

"Stella!" Herb is standing, wide-eyed with horror. "Were they *here?*"

She waves him off with an imperious gesture. "You like to tell your stories in detail; now let me tell mine."

"But Stella, dearest — "

"She's right," interposed Hilda McCool annoyedly. "You get mad whenever anyone interrupts *you.*"

Stella Frobisher continues in utter frankness:

"Would you believe it — oh, stupid me! — when the three men walked up our path, in black leather jackets and tight blue denim pants, they looked so tired and innocent it never even entered my mind — "

"Stella!" — Herb's anguished voice — "Tell me! Tell me what happened!"

His wife gives him a withering look. "I never even suspected, when the big one asked if he could come in and get a drink of water, it might be a trick . . . "

"STELLA!"

Herb is now slumped over the stuffed sofa arm, distraught.

"Too much punch again," says Hilda McCool, regarding him coldly. "It's a shame."

Stella goes on, "They told me they were actors from New Jersey, hoping for a break with the Old Barn Playhouse up the river."

"Did one of them have a cute little black moustache?" Hilda asks with interest. "The youngest one?"

"Yes," says Stella. "Sort of cute, but scraggly."

"STELLA!"

But by now no one is paying attention to Herb, who is prone on the floor, pounding his forehead on the hardwood. It's a shame.

"And who were they?" Hilda asks avidly. "Tell us every little bit of it!"

"They were actors from New Jersey," Stella replies. "I gave them chicken sandwiches and coffee, and they showed me their clippings. My, were they ever nice boys!"

After all the guests leave, a strange thing happens. Herb, for some reason seeming unaccountably abject and gasping for words, tells Stella he is going to sell the country cottage and buy her a mink coat with the proceeds if she will just be content to stay in town.

It's peculiar the extremes men will go to when they find they are not as good story-tellers as their wives.

A Good Rest
at Home

Nothing cures a man's cold more quickly than a good rest at home.

Everyone at the office will assure you of this when you start sneezing over them, and they will push you out the door with admonitions to take care of yourself, refrain from worrying about how things are going, and stay away until you feel completely well.

Once outside, a new spring comes into your stride. A day in the luxury of bed — perhaps two days. That's the life! You can see yourself propped up with a good book, nibbling a lunch served on a bed tray by a devoted wife. She is whispering to the youngsters peering in the doorway, "Sh-h-h-h! — Father is very ill."

Just as you pictured it, she meets you worriedly at the door. But here, right at the outset, she misses her cue entirely. Where she should say, "You poor dear; let me help you up the steps," she says, "Well what did you forget this time?"

"I'm a sick man."

"Sick! You don't look sick. What's the matter with you?" This wasn't in the script, either.

"I have an awful (cough, cough) cold."

"Oh, for heaven's sake. You scared me. You haven't half as bad a cold as I've got. Wait — where do you think you're going?"

"Up to bed (cough, cough)."

"You can't do that — I just made your bed. Lie on the chesterfield if you think you have to lie down."

You turn on the TV, and lie down, and she reappears hauling the vacuum cleaner. "Move to the armchair; I'll do the chesterfield first so you can move back."

You sit down. The vacuum cleaner makes the TV roar.

33

You get up and turn the set off. You sit down. The chair feels very comfortable. You get up and go back to the chesterfield so she can do the chair. You get up and go back to the chair. You lift one foot, then the other, so she can do the carpet. You get up so she can move the chair and do the carpet.

You give up and plod aimlessly out to the kitchen, pausing to warn your three-year-old son off the second-floor bannister. Reaching the kitchen, you hear your wife scream, and you sprint back expecting the worst has happened. You find her saying, "Mummy told you never to pick the leaves off her plants."

You shuffle back to the kitchen, wishing you had something to do. You decide to try prying the lid off a balky paint can, by tapping the lid with an old knife while holding the can on the stove, and a voice says: "Don't do that, please; I've a cake rising in the oven." This makes no sense to a husband, but only a husband with no sense will question it.

As you shuffle out of the kitchen again, the three children tag along, asking you to play barber. This is a game they made up three months ago, the last time you took a midday nap, and the gaps in your hair are still growing back. You say no.

You get down on all fours to see what the lower bookshelves contain, as you forgot to bring home that good book. The result consists of *Orations Delivered at Saint John's Loyalist Centennial, 1883, The Outdoor Girls at Lake Winneehassee* (1916), and three children climbing on your back and vigorously pummelling you to giddap.

A minute later, locking yourself in the cellar, you hopefully begin *The Outdoor Girls*:

Sarah stood pensively on the diving-board, scanning the end of the lake for the steamer. "Oh, please, dear Bluebell, please hurry up!" she exclaimed impetuously. "If you don't arrive soon I shall die of quiet exasperation." She looked down at her mischievous friend Gladys, who was washing her middie and making impish faces at her. "Sarah," the fun-loving girl said with a ringing laugh, "do stop fretting. For my part I shall not care if the dad-blamed boat never comes." Sarah, who was wearing her only pressed pair of bloomers,

nearly fell into the water in astonishment. "Please!" she re-
plied earnestly. "You will regret your new slang expressions
if Camp Mother Brewster hears, and then you cannot be
Sequoia Maiden at the Starlight Ceremony."

You close the dad-blamed book in quiet exasperation,
trudge up the stairs, and leave for the office, noticing pleasur-
ably that the further away you get from the house the better
you feel.

Yes, nothing cures a man's cold more quickly than a good
rest at home. Often it cures colds for years to come.

The Case of
the Disappearing
Den

There's a peculiar thing about house plans that puzzles most of the men I know.

On the blueprints of the homes they build, they see a word as plain as anything: "DEN."

This lettering usually materializes on a small room off a hall — just the kind of cosy nook where a man can cherish his books and his pipe and relax in perfect peace.

I'm certain it helps to convince many husbands that for the sake of the wife and the kids it's time they had a home of their own.

But when the house is finished — *presto!* The room isn't there!

What happened to it? Where did it go?

Was it sheer wishful thinking all the time — a self-induced mirage? Or is this some sort of optical illusion — a diabolical sleight-of-hand — that architects use to lure prospective clients?

"I was just about to move my microscope table into the room," said my bewildered friend Bill Bartley, "when I found the dog's bed in one corner, the canary cage in another, and a lot of dresses hanging in the closet. I asked Hilda about it — she was there, too, sewing on the sewing machine — and she said I must be crazy; she'd never heard of any 'den' in the plans. She calls it 'the sewing room.' The kids call it 'the dog's room.'"

My neighbor Herb Frobisher was equally baffled. He put up a lovely $45,000 ranch house, thinking the den would be just the spot for poring over his stamp collection.

"I'm positive I saw 'DEN' on the plans," he told me, but I could see he already doubted his own powers of recollection.

"I distinctly remember — or I think I do — telling Stella I could even put a cot in there and snooze whenever I felt like it."

"And then," I prompted, "you started to move your stamp collection in, and you found the sewing machine — "

"Yes, yes," he cried excitedly. "That was it! How did you know? The sewing machine was there, and — "

"And the dog's bed?"

"*Dog*?" he laughed hollowly. "We don't have a dog. But there was the cat's bed, and the sewing machine, and the washer and dryer — they were there just temporarily — and I said to Stella, 'Isn't this supposed to be my den?' "

"And," I broke in, "she said, 'What den? I don't recall any den.' "

"Exactly!" he exclaimed — and then, deflatedly, "Oh . . . you must have been talking with Stella; you know all about it. Anyway, I was *sure* there was a den, and all the while I must have been looking at some other blueprint!"

I feel sorry for these husbands. I know the folly of planning to build a house with a den in it. That was why, when we decided to move to a bigger house, I picked one already built, where I could walk right in and impress upon everyone in the family that *this* was to be my den and no question about it.

That's the whole trick: Settle it definitely before you move in!

I carried my stuff into the room myself — desk, typewriter, lamp, books, bookcase — to make sure where they went.

I didn't budge one iota from my desk, where I was writing a letter, when my wife pushed the sewing machine in, saying, "You're not going to need the whole room right at the start, are you?"

Nor did I stir off my chair when the dresses came in, followed by Karl, our hundred-pound German shepherd, with his bed, and the cat and her newborn kittens and their box, and then the spool bed and the dresser, in case company arrived. ("We could always call it our 'spare room' for one night," my wife said.)

You see, I've stuck to my rights.

I happen to be typing these words just now in the basement — not because I've given up the den permanently, you understand, but only because when my cousin-in-law and his wife came to stay, they found it difficult to go to bed while I was typing in the same room.

But I'll be right back up there, tomorrow when they leave! My wife definitely promised me that only a few minutes ago, when she hurried down to get some potatoes.

She also mumbled something about moving our younger boy, who seems to be coming down with chickenpox, away from our older boy; but I don't get it. We don't have another bedroom.

Could I See
a Good Murder?

"Professionally trained librarians," says a news item I'm read-ing, *"are very scarce. It is difficult to encourage young people to enter the field. They think it must be a dull and inactive life."*

That's certainly absurd. Why, public librarians enjoy a more active life than anybody else. I know. I've seen them enjoying it.

This being Library Week, let's just look in on the hushed reading-room of a typical mid-Victorian library in a typical mid-Canadian town.

Old Mr. Beskwith, who drifts off to sleep while reading, often talks in his dreams. Today he lets out merely a loud whoop: "HEY! STOP!" This wakes him up again. Everyone turns and stares. He stares back, puzzled — he didn't say any-thing.

The librarian, Miss McQuill, comes running. She in-quires earnestly in his ear, "Are you all right?" He looks up: "Why, sure." He is a little huffed. He doesn't see why she's always asking him; lots of other people in the room look sicker than he does.

An assistant librarian hurries in, whispers to her, "The Reverend's up again." This electrifies Miss McQuill. She dashes out, and up a steel stairway to a second-floor platform of book racks where an elderly man is grasping the railing, teetering.

"I want to see a good murder," he explains as she grabs his bony arm.

Miss McQuill knows that. He reads one every day. She finds them for him. Unfortunately, if she seems busy, the kindly old gentleman gropes up the stairway himself, then feels too dizzy to come down again.

"Could I see a good murder?" he reiterates as they stumble

together off the final step. "You will," she mutters under her breath, "if you do that once more."

From the reading-room, suddenly — "GIT, DOG! GIT!"

"Here, hold this!" says Miss McQuill, handing the Reverend's arm to an assistant for safekeeping. She sprints, but she knows there isn't a dog in there; only old Mr. Beskwith. She starts over to speak to him, sighs, then changes her mind. He is glaring at her over his newspaper. He knows what she's thinking of, and he's getting pretty fed up with it. She's thinking of making a public spectacle of him again.

"Many young people," the news item goes on, *"reject the idea of a methodical library job in favor of a more competitive calling, one where they will have to match wits with their fellows."*

There's just the point! If young people only knew it, librarians do more wit-matching than anybody.

Just look at Miss McQuill as she tiptoes down a line of backroom book racks, stopping to flick a speck of dust off. Is she dusting? Not a bit of it: She's hot on the trail of a common library halfwit — the man who rubs out bad words with a hard ink eraser. She's matching wits with him.

An assistant taps her shoulder: "Miss McQuill — Miss McQuill! We've just found three more books in the next room with words rubbed out. Two with whole chapters torn out. And somebody has written all over the pages of a religious book!"

Poor Miss McQuill. At the desk, more exciting news awaits her: "While you were gone, somebody cut three more slips off the begonia."

Oddly enough, Miss McQuill doesn't even cast a suspicious glance at the Reverend's wife who is patiently waiting for him near the desk — even though she is known to be an African violet enthusiast. This is possibly due to the fact that last Christmas, when they were all so sure she was the guilty party, the librarians sardonically presented her with one of the library's small potted begonias.

The good woman gasped with elation: "I've never had a begonia in the house before." And, it turned out on later investigation, neither she had.

The only problem now is what to do next Christmas. The Reverend's wife will be expecting something again. I understand Miss McQuill is planning to give her one of the potted ferns — if the library commissioners don't find out about it first.

"Youth today wants a career that constantly opens up new vistas, new opportunities, new mental challenges."

Well, if there are any better mental challenges than trying to figure out the book titles library customers ask for, I haven't heard of them.

Watch Miss McQuill. Nothing rattles her. A meek-looking middle-aged man sidles up, half-glancing around as if expecting to see his wife materialize at his elbow. He whispers, "Do you have *Leona?* I'm not sure — it may be *Lorelei*."

"Sorry, sir," says Miss McQuill without hesitation. "We didn't get *Lolita*."

"Oh, thank you very much," says the man, a silly look of embarrassment on his face as he fades around the corner of the book racks.

With the same equanimity, Miss McQuill fulfills requests for *"Doctor Chicago,* I think it is," *Anatomy of a Murderer* and *The Man in the Long Gray Flannel Underwear*.

"All young people interviewed had the impression the librarian's life is not sufficiently rewarding."

I don't know what money librarians make. But there are other rewards. Why, most people almost never fail to enclose a present with the books they return.

Miss McQuill has a cigar box half full of goodwill tokens that have fallen unexpectedly out of the pages — numerous bobby pins, several snapshots of young men squeezing laughing girls, six unpaid bills, two blank cheques, a dog show best-of-breed ribbon.

"Once," she muses nostalgically, "we found a $10 bill." Of course, the owner returned for that.

Miss McQuill also remembers reading that a U.S. library once found a strip of bacon in a book. There's originality for you — a bookmark that can be eaten while you read!

"One college girl said, 'I'd be afraid to be a librarian. I might become a frozen-faced old maid.'"

This is the height of absurdity. That fearsome falcon-eye librarian stare she remembers from her childhood — that was all put on! Librarians assumed the look on purpose — in self-defence — like school teachers. They had to intimidate people.

I know, myself. Once, as a boy, I heard an ominous whisper over my shoulder: "Are you eating something?" In desperation to hide it, I clenched my teeth tight on a two-for-a-cent chewy molasses candy known as a honeymoon. They stuck.

"Are you eating something?"

I couldn't answer. I hoped they would think I was dumb, but the assistant asked me to leave. It was, I thought, a pretty poor way to treat a dumb boy — especially when I was such a regular patron of the reference room, as all my classmates were. You see, word had got around our school that the city library possessed a huge Oxford dictionary set — a volume about the size of a family Bible for each letter — with every bad word defined in full glorious detail, including Shakespearean and other classical examples of its use. The whole class went to gain a new appreciation of the Bard. As we certainly raised the attendance figures at the library that year, it seemed to me a burning injustice to be put out merely for eating honeymoons, especially when I hadn't even finished the "B" volume yet. I haven't got over the experience yet; it has given me a complex.

Everywhere you'll see countless inhibited victims as the result of such childhood experiences — casualties of an era when libraries were solemn cathedrals of literary worship.

Watch a gaggle of middle-aged clubwomen straggling into Miss McQuill's library. As they open the massive door, they are still shrieking and chortling. . . . "But if Betty won't tell him herself, then who on earth — "

Sudden silence. They shuffle in red-faced, bumping into one another, each prodding the other to go ahead first — as if they'd opened a wrong door and found themselves in the midst of a funeral service.

The truth is, they're little girls again.

"The consensus was that students want a job 'right in the

know' of what's going on in their community, with lots of chance to meet stimulating people."

"What's going on" — is that what they want to know? Then who knows better than the librarian? Miss McQuill can tell you immediately, for instance, when a depression is coming without even looking out the window: People start reading a phenomenal number of books. It's a sure portent.

If you're not interested in depressions, she can tell you — but she won't — exactly who in town is going to have a baby. She knows even before the relatives do. It always happens the same way: A recent bride comes in and asks, crimson-faced: "Do you have any books on painless childbirth? A friend of mine asked me to get her one."

Friends of recent brides, it seems, are particularly susceptible to maternity.

As for "stimulating people" — where else but in a public library could you meet anyone as stimulating as old Mr. Beskwith? When he gives a sudden shout, "DON'T ROLL OVER ON ME," everyone in the reading-room jumps a foot.

Running neck and neck with him is the Reverend. No one else can keep so many librarians running.

I must say I envy him, in a way. I envy all clergymen in a public library. No matter what they ask for, other patrons praise them to the skies. If they suggest a humor book, it shows the warm human side of their nature. If they want an adventure story, they long for the broader horizons they cannot have; if hot stuff, they merely want to keep track of what the younger people are reading.

Today he is bringing back *Lady Chatterly's Lover*. Somehow, he explains, he got hold of it by mistake; he didn't know what kind of a book it was. If I said that, Miss McQuill would think it was a weak excuse. But in the Reverend's case, they understand it immediately: The good man thought, naturally, that Lady Chatterly's Lover must be Lord Chatterly.

A middle-aged man and his wife, who evidently used to be his parishioners, tiptoe over and greet him effusively. They talk — as middle-aged people in a library always do — in stage whispers that carry all over the building, disturbing everyone, even though they themselves can't understand what they are saying to each other.

The woman nudges her husband in a sharp aside: "Keep that book under your arm. Don't let the Reverend see you read cheap murders."

Then the Reverend quavers loudly, "I'd like to see a good murder, please."

The woman whispers to her husband, "Isn't he a fine man! — likes to keep his brain as nimble as the next fellow."

And out they go, still whispering, into the strange raucous world where people shout across the street and automobile horns bleat as if they didn't even know they were making such an ear-splitting din.

Maneuvers
in the
Barber Shop

Maybe I'm old-fashioned, but it always frightens me to step into a streamlined barber shop. My appearance is the signal for a hurried butting of cigarettes and a scramble of nine white-uniformed barbers to their chairs, nearly bowling me over in the rush for action stations.

Then, standing at rigid attention, they watch my every move. The uncomfortable feeling persists that with their high side-button collars they look like nine doctors eager to open me up.

The tense silence aggravates my nervousness. I can't seem to hang up my hat on the hook so it will stay — quite a trick, with nine pairs of eyes watching — until in desperation I drive it on so hard the hook goes through the felt.

Now comes the terrifying climax: I have to turn and face the expectant white line. I wish I had the nerve to stroll along the motionless row like a general reviewing troops and climb into the chair of the ninth barber, who gets a customer only when the first eight are busy and at other times just gets the exercise of scrambling.

But I haven't any nerve at all, which provokes me with myself. I don't dare pass even one of them; he may think I don't like his haircuts. But neither can I simply walk to the nearest chair, or they will think I have no willpower. So I stare absentmindedly at my feet in embarrassment, and walk in the general direction of all nine. When I see a blurry white shape loom up, I say, "Oh! Good morning," and clamber into his chair, hoping the others will think I didn't notice they were there.

Unfortunately, I always walk to the same barber. He is the one I dread. I mumble, "A little trim, please," and he says, "Yes, *sir!*" and enthusiastically attacks me with the shears.

Even after I practise at home turning and walking in different directions with my eyes shut, I still walk straight to him. I'm certain he keeps changing chairs on me.

Not for several moments after settling in his chair do I lift my eyes from my lap to the mirror to see whether the other barbers, who have broken ranks and dispersed, are looking at me resentfully because of my favoritism. They don't *seem* to be. One is showing his sports page to another, who is reading a girdle ad; but this could be camouflage. He may be whispering I'm not the tipping kind anyway, while the other is saying I've let my hair grow so long the job isn't worth it. In a way, I'm glad I can't lip-read.

It appears to do me no good to peer in the shop window from the street first to make sure the enthusiastic barber has already got somebody else's head at his mercy. When he sees me coming in he always speeds up anyway in anticipation, because he thinks he owns me. Then one of the other barbers finishes a haircut and goes to lunch. Another leaves for the bank to get some change. Another is called to the phone. I am trapped: my old friend decides there's nothing more left on his customer's head worth whittling off, and I am next.

You say why don't I try a small shop? I *did*. I started at Mr. Smedley's, where the haircuts were 65 cents. Mr. Smedley kept a second man, an old itinerant barber named Ben, to make himself look better by comparison.

Ben could easily remember Ty Cobb's batting average for 1913, but never could remember how I wore my hair when I got into his chair twenty minutes before. He clipped the sides off completely, because that's how he liked his own hair and he believed in doing unto others as he would other barbers unto him; he sliced up the top in assorted slab lengths, moved the part over to the middle, curved it around the base of the skull and asked me how *that* was.

I could only nod agreeably or Ben's feelings would be hurt, and the waiting customers glancing up from their magazines to inspect each finished product would think I was vain.

On leaving the shop, I hurried to the nearest men's washroom, keeping my hat on till I got there, and tried to change

46

the part before anyone asked me who was throwing the Gay Nineties party. But that's where old Ben had me: the patching-up was useless. His talent was in the fact he cut hair with such unconscious ingenuity that I had to leave his handiwork untouched or the hair would jut out everywhere like the eaves of a thatched hut.

So all the customers always told Ben, "I'm waiting for Mr. Smedley." Time after time Ben's face lighted up when a customer came in, but even though Mr. Smedley was already busily snipping, and four or five people were waiting, the newcomer announced, "I'm waiting for Mr. Smedley." You could tell he'd been there before.

I never had the heart to say it — even though I knew that letting Ben at me would prompt friends to exclaim for days afterwards, as though it was news, "You've had a haircut."

One day I almost worked up the courage — the day the kitchen water pipes froze and I was furious with everybody except myself. But I faltered at the crucial moment and climbed meekly into Ben's chair. This made me so furious with myself I never went back.

Then I tried a three-chair shop that offered haircuts at the same price, 65 cents. When I saw how obliging the head barber was, I realized I should have switched years ago. The conversation went like this:

"*There* you are, sir. And now a little dash of lemon on the hair roots?" "Well, I don't mind if I do, if you don't mind." "A little Flexicreem around the ears? Great for the ears." "Why, that's very good of you." "A drop of Egyptian Balsam to nourish healthy follicles?" "Yes, certainly, if it's not too much bother." It wasn't. When he finished, I gave him a dollar bill and started out the door.

"Hey!" he said, smiling, holding up the bill. "You forgot something."

"That's all right," I said, smiling back. "Keep the change." I thought he deserved it.

"But you only gave me the *tip*," he laughed. "You forgot the haircut and treatments. They come to $5.85."

The other barbers and the customers and myself joined in a great guffaw over my forgetfulness. There was a lot of good-natured kidding. Someone remembered a famous character of twenty years before who always tried to get out without paying and someone else suggested hilariously they had better see if I had any towels in my pocket. One thing I *did* remember, however, was not to go back.

Nor could I go back now to Mr. Smedley and old Ben, as I would be unable to offer them a satisfactory explanation of where I got my last haircut. I couldn't face the unspoken question in their eyes. I still duck into doorways when I see one of them coming, and hope they think I have died or moved away.

That was how I moved up into the nine-chair modern three-dollar barber shop at the airport, where the barbers carry out tactical drill borrowed from the army and wear high-necked tunics borrowed from the doctors — the ones in the laxative ads, with miners' lights on their foreheads — while real-life doctors, to make their patients feel at ease, try to look as informal as barbers did before *they* began trying to look like doctors.

Christmas
Joy

Yule Greetings
Yule Never Get

The happy, happy season of Christmas cards is upon us again. Isn't it wonderful to see them pouring in? Gay, glittering messengers of good cheer — how I love to read them!

I love to send them, too — they spread so much joy!

The only slight trouble is, the ones I send seem to conspire against me. They know my failings; they delight in outwitting me. I don't know why. I think it's because they're young and irrepressible — fresh out of the factory.

For instance, I discover a card with an attractive holly-and-cherub design on a store counter. I like it.

"I'll take a dozen of these."

"Twelve?" The busy clerk looks at me strangely.

"No — wait. Make it two dozen!"

"Twenty-four?"

"Yes, please" — irritably. Doesn't she think I know twenty-four people?

It's not until I get home and admire them again, with my glasses on, that I notice a fine line of script has appeared under the cherub: "To My Dear Sweet Mother-In-Law."

You see? It wasn't there when I bought them. That's a trick Christmas cherubs are always playing on me.

The rollicking little tykes also love to hide where I can't find them. In fact, half a dozen expensive angel cards — ones I'd bought for my best friends — disappeared right off our dining room table this year. I looked everywhere for them.

"I can't understand it," I told my wife. "I distinctly recall putting them there early Friday evening. Remember? You were just sitting down to send a few cards to your relatives."

My wife can't understand it either.

All I can say is that grown-up angels with halos, as far as mischievousness is concerned, are just as bad as cherubs, choir boys, pixies or reindeer.

50

But the cards don't start their horseplay in earnest until I begin addressing them. This is a big job. The proper systematic method calls for the new boxes and the lists from past years to be spread carefully over the dining-room table on a quiet Sunday afternoon, as it's important to select the right card for the right person. Sheets of stamps and a telephone book should be at your left hand, the pile of greetings you received last year at your right hand. Once you get the knack of it, you can finish all your cards in one afternoon!

I begin with high hopes, picking the first card from last year's pile: "Warmest Christmas Wishes — from Bill and Mary, 262 Gleeside Street, Arnprior, Ont."

I frown at it in puzzlement.

"Who are Bill and Mary?" I call out to the kitchen.

"Bill and Mary who?"

"That's what I want to know! They sent us a card last year from Arnprior."

"Oh. The Nerffs! Mr. and Mrs. William Nerff."

I pick out a laughing-cherub card I never liked anyway; it doesn't matter, as they are friends of my wife's.

I write on the envelope: Mr. and Mrs. William Nerff, 262 Gleeside . . . .

"They moved to Timmins," adds the helpful voice from the kitchen, "last July."

I crumple the envelope.

The light-hearted Christmas cards seem to be mocking me from their boxes. They always love this. It counts one point for them; the object of their game is to see how many cards they can make me have left over, without envelopes.

"*Whereabouts* in Timmins?"

"You could phone her sister Aggie; she'd know."

I find Aggie at home; this is my lucky day!

Eyeing the silly-looking cherub, I start to address another envelope. My wife asks:

"Did you remember to buy stamps?"

"Yes" — distractedly — "four dollars' worth."

To my dismay I look at what the miserable cherub has made me write:

"Mr. and Mrs. William Stamps."

I grab a third envelope. Silently I vow to get it right this time, no matter what.

"Have you seen the screwdriver, Dad?" my son's voice hollers from the back hall.

"It's on the shelf."

I begin to write as I answer him, with one eye on the devilish cherub. I'm grimly determined not to put down "screwdriver" or "shelf" or "Dad." I'm too smart this time; I'm going to get it right.

Suddenly the words stare back at me:

"Mr. and Mrs. William Right."

In desperation, to regain my composure, I drop in to see if Herb Frobisher is doing anything interesting. He's counting up his Christmas-card names. He's frantic. He's cussing everybody on the list.

"What do they think I am?" — flinging the list in my general direction — "A millionaire? Look at the new people who sent us cards last year — 32 of them! This year I'll have to send out 140. Next year it'll be 170. Soon I'll be sending to everyone in the world!"

He buries his face in his arms.

Feeling much better for some reason, I return to grapple with the Nerffs. To my relief, I write the address perfectly!

Then my heart sinks. Concentrating so hard on the words, I've written the lines too high. There's no room for the stamp.

"How are you getting along?" — cheerily from the kitchen.

"Me? Oh, fine!"

I'm deep in perplexity, but a woman wouldn't under-stand it. I *could* squeeze a stamp on it, by covering up the "Nerff." But what if the postman didn't have sense enough to look under the stamp? Would he insist on hunting all over Timmins for Mr. and Mrs. William? On a happy inspiration, I bend the stamp over the top of the envelope, as though I absent-mindedly thought I was putting a sticker on a present for them. It's good enough for those trouble-makers.

A knock on the front door. In comes, slowly, Bill Bartley. I'm delighted. This is a real break. Bill's always a barrel of fun.

52

Bill doesn't look like himself. He's bent over. His face is twisted.

"Just hoped you'd cheer me up," he gasps, holding his back. "Been writing Christmas cards for four hours. *Ow!*"

As he eases himself into a chair, my wife breezes by from the kitchen. "Don't forget the Thirstles out in Wisconsin! They were the people on the plane, remember? They sent us one last year."

"Those old idiots?" I grumble — and then, hopefully, "Perhaps they've died."

"I wouldn't bother with the fools," mutters Bill, who doesn't even know them.

"And better put a nice friendly letter in with the card to the Carsons," the blithe voice calls from the living room "They didn't send us one last year."

"A *letter?*"

"Cross 'em off," growls Bill Bartley, who doesn't know them, either.

Fortunately, just when I'm getting mad at the Carsons for expecting me to do all this extra work, Walter Holburn stumbles in. He looks ghastly pale. He's bushed.

"Would you fellows come down to the club with me?" He sounds pitiful. "When I went last year, the wife finished up all my Christmas cards."

Bill and I both go, just to help poor Walter.

Amazingly, when I come home only two hours later, practically all my cards are done, too!

My wife has left me only an assortment of six to finish. This is a cinch; now that the end is in sight, I can really roll. But what a diabolical way those cards re-sort themselves when they see who's back on the job! I address the top card; it's perfect for Aunt Elspeth. The next just suits Cousin Frank. But the very last card, for Great-Aunt Prue, the last name on our list — wouldn't you know it has cleverly concealed itself on the bottom all this time?

It shows two cocktail glasses clinking — "A Toast To The Gayest Bang-Up Season Yet!"

Dazedly I dig into an old box of leftovers. Only one card, out of twenty, has an envelope. It's a smiling cow jumping over the moon — "The Sky's The Limit, Kid — Get A Big Kick Out Of New Year's!" It's the one I couldn't send her last year.

Once again I decide it's easier to give Great-Aunt Prue a potted African violet.

I'm thankful, at least, to know that the merry-making Christmas cards have had done with me — that I've finished them before they finished me.

But walking to the post office, an awful feeling comes over me: Didn't I forget to sign one card? The obsession grows. It takes all my will power not to go back and steam them open — also the memory that last year they laughed at me, they were all signed, every one.

After I mail them, too, I get a strange sensation: Did I forget to put a stamp on one of the envelopes? I bang on the iron postal wicket until the clerk comes. He looks familiar. He listens to me tight-lipped, goes over to a huge receptacle and checks through its contents.

"Well," he finally comes back and sighs, "they all have stamps," then adds mysteriously, with the strange look I've seen on some postal clerks, "just like they had last year."

As I trudge homeward, I never want to see a Christmas card again.

The astonishing thing is how all this is forgotten when our own Christmas cards start coming in, including a very nice one from Mr. and Mrs. Thirstle in Wisconsin. How personally selected they all obviously are! Every pretty design, every gladsome greeting, has clearly been chosen just for us. We can almost imagine each happy sender saying the hearty words to us!

It just shows, I guess, that nobody else goes through what the Frobishers and the Bartleys and the Holburns and ourselves do every December.

Odd, though, about the Nerffs' greeting. They didn't send us a card at all — the envelope just had a grocery list in it. It's ingenious, I know, but I don't get it. Why should they tell us what they like to eat? All I can figure is that they're planning to visit us soon.

The Christmas Ties
That Bind

Christmas is the observance of countless individual family customs. These cherished and time-honored traditions, unfailingly carried on from year to year, really make the occasion.

It's a lovely thought.

How true it is!

I know, because all my friends observe different Christmas customs. For instance, every Christmas Eve around midnight, unfailingly, I get a phone call from Herb Frobisher:

"Hi! Howsha boy?"

His voice sounds strangely slurred. This is due, I believe, to the heavy use of the lines Christmas Eve.

"Fine, fine," I always say. "How are you, Herb?"

"Shwell!" — exuberantly as if he's surprised and delighted to find himself feeling so well. "Having shimply wunnerful party! Howsha like to come?"

When I decline, he seems puzzled; he's taken aback. But he's patient with my contrariness. He repeats the invitation thickly several times, in different ways, apparently under the impression my mind isn't very clear tonight and if he can only get the idea through to me I'll jump at the chance.

Finally I manage to convince him I can't go out — I still have the tree to do.

"Thash awful," he says slowly, sadly. "No tree up." Herb's a very sympathetic fellow. He's deeply touched. He sounds on the verge of tears.

I've hardly hung up when Stella Frobisher phones. She asks anxiously:

"Have you seen Herb?"

"No" — in surprise. "Isn't he home?"

She snorts. "Just wait till I lay my hands on that bum — 12 o'clock and our tree still lying out here on the veranda!"

No sooner is she off the line than the phone tingles again. It's Herb. He's provoked. He sounds righteously angry with me.

"Washa matter? Wash keepin' you?" he demands. "Are you a shpoil-shport?"

I explain it all over again, adding, "Listen, are you at home?"

He laughs raucously.

"Boy — am I *ever*! If there'sh one thing I feel, ish *very* mush at home!"

In the background I can hear glasses tinkling, giggling squeals, high-pitched screams.

"Hey, you want shome help?" he suggests on a sudden inspiration. "You want ush all come and put up your old tree?"

I hang up hurriedly, hoping the thought will go out of his mind.

The phone jangles again, startlingly. I lift the receiver and begin, "Now, look here . . ."

"What did you say? Who on earth are you talking to?" It's Stella Frobisher's sharp voice. "Is Herb with you?"

"No; he's home."

"*Home?*" — an incredulous gasp.

"Yes; I was just talking with him. Where are you?"

"I know where I'm *going* to be. In the nuthouse!"

Thank goodness, when Herb rings again, the thought *has* gone out of his mind. It's blank. He begins brightly:

"Hi! Howsha boy?"

"Fine, fine, Herb. How are you?"

"Shwell! Shay, howsha like come to a shimply wunnerful party?"

They're a funny couple, Herb and Stella. They make calls like this every Christmas Eve, just to get a rise out of me, I think. I'm sure it's all joking, because neither ever mentions it afterward.

The wrestling match at Bill Bartley's house — between Bill and his wife Hilda — is another distinctive Christmas custom.

Oh, they don't wrestle each other; they're not silly. They wrestle with the tree. Bill wants to put it up, and Hilda wants to keep it down. They both wrestle with the tree at the same time, shouting at each other, "No you don't!"

Bill comes from a family that always trimmed its tree a week before Christmas. This was very sensible. Callers during the pre-Christmas week were received in an appropriate festive atmosphere.

Hilda's family *never* put the tree up before Christmas Eve, quite sensibly, too, because then the full impact of Christmas was felt by the children getting up in the morning.

I can tell you, they put on quite an act — it's all just harmless horseplay, of course. When Bill hoists the tree upright, smiling genially at me and saying, "Guess it's about time I started on this job," Hilda jumps up and grabs the trunk, pulling strenuously and retorting, "You quit that! You needn't think you can run on me just because you have company!" She smiles genially in my direction, too, to show she's really good-natured, and then pulls, and kicks him in the stomach, and he swears.

When Hilda finds Bill has sneakily got the tree up and is starting to decorate it from a step-ladder, I've seen her drag it down with such a yank that Bill came too, sprawling over the floor.

"Oh, my nose!" he wailed. "I think you've broken my nose!"

"I hope it swells up good and big," she said. "It'll remind you not to try that again."

If you didn't know them as well as I do, and what fine people they are, you'd be sure they were in earnest.

It even fooled their kids. They clustered around their father, who was holding his nose, pleading, "*Please* don't put the tree up again, Daddy!"

The cloak-and-dagger game at the Frewleys' is a Christmas tradition I especially envy. It enlivens the season for both of them, and doesn't cost a cent.

Bert Frewley comes from a family that always opened its Christmas cards, naturally, just as soon as they were received.

But in Eudice Frewley's home the cards were always saved intact in their envelopes to be opened ceremoniously on Christmas morning.

What a happy competition this leads to!

Both run out to the gate to meet the postman, demanding the cards, Bert so he can open them quick, Eudice so she can hide them away under the girdles, foam-rubber bustle and pony-tails of false hair in her lowest bureau drawer (the one Bert isn't supposed to look into).

"Give them to me. I've *got* to see them," Bert appeals to the postman. "There may be somebody we should send one back to!"

"Don't you dare," Eudice commands the postman; "they're addressed to me, too!"

The only person who doesn't enter into the spirit of the game is the postman. I'm sorry to say he lacks courage. When he sees them sprinting from the house, both shouting at him and jostling each other with their elbows, he throws the cards over the hedge and runs.

Poor Bert! I've been at his house evenings when Eudice is at her bridge club; it's a weird experience to watch him furtively opening her unsealed envelopes and marking down who sent the cards. When he thinks he hears her coming — any alley cat upsetting a garbage can cover can throw Bert into a panic — it's nerve-wracking to see the frantic scramble to get them back into their proper envelopes and shove them under the girdles. In his haste Bert often stuffs some *inside* the girdles. He can never understand afterwards how Eudice knows what he was up to. He thinks she has psychic feelings.

Many's the night I've held a flashlight for Bert in his darkened living room — an eight-cell flashlight, with a powerful beam — so he can try to read the cards that are in sealed envelopes.

He curses the senders for their lack of thoughtfulness.

"How can they expect me to know who sent them," he asks with undeniable logic, "if they lick the envelopes and close them?"

"It's ridiculous, all right," I agree. "Serve them right if they don't get any back."

My friends have all sorts of other wonderful Christmas customs, too:

There's the Billings' annual amusing Christmas Eve

58

tug-of-war over where to hang the stockings (he's a fireplace man; she's a bedpost girl).

There's the spectacle of Mr. Mitton jumping up from the Christmas dinner table every year, gagging, and snapping on the light switch and roaring, "This is the end! No more candlelight in this house!" Of course, it's his own fault. He never can remember that the butter isn't the cream cheese until he cuts himself a slice and swallows it.

There's the mausoleum-like silence that enshrouds the Thurwell residence Christmas Day, due to the fact Mr. Thurwell is inside alone, sulking. He adamantly refuses to budge out of doors that day, as it's a time for family happiness. His wife, who was brought up to regard Christmas as the time for neighborly visits, is out somewhere being neighborly.

There's the Hopleys' unique Christmas tree, trimmed on one side with popcorn strings and gauze candy bags, as he insists on, and with angel's hair and tinsel icicles on the other, to satisfy her. It's an amicable compromise, especially so as each thinks it's spoiling Christmas for the other.

And there's the unvarying custom of Judge Barthitt, who stalks to the club to spend Christmas night in angry solitude. I must say he has good reason, though it is not generally known. His wife has refused again to fill a stocking for him.

Thank goodness, my wife and I agree perfectly on Christmas customs. There is the small point, of course, that she wants a little tree on a table, and I always favor a huge tree, cut off at the top, which seems to go through the ceiling. (Isn't it lovely to smell that nostalgic balsam fragrance as soon as you enter a house?) And some day we *are* going to have a tree like that.

Smile,
Darn You, Kiddies -
You Too, Rover!

More happy Christmas family gatherings will be preserved on film this year than ever before.

Everybody's taking pictures. It's wonderful fun!

In case you are new to the hobby, you can get quite a few valuable pointers from our neighborhood experience.

First, remember that everyone is on a conspiracy to thwart you. This may seem strange, but it's a well-known fact among amateur cameramen. Even the smallest children know, probably by instinct, the game is to foil your plans.

My friend Herb Frobisher is convinced of this. Last Christmas he got out his color-slide camera after the festive dinner and told the assorted relatives cheerily:

"Everybody over by the Christmas tree to get their picture taken!"

This was a signal for the babies to crawl behind the sofa, for two toddlers to want a drink of water, for a nephew to pull his cousin's hair, for her to chase and kick him, for his wife to say just a minute while she went to turn off the stove, for his son to run to the front door to let the dog in.

In a twinkling the living room was bare.

When he finally corralled them, they stood stiffly in a wooden group, glowering at him. This, Herb believes, was all part of the conspiracy. His wife Stella contended it was because their faces reflected his own anxious frown — the way young choirs unconsciously mimic their director's expression at a music festival — but Herb knows of course she was wrong, because he's always the soul of geniality.

"No, smile!" he ordered them, his voice rising. "For heaven's sake, smile, *smile!*"

They obliged, but for some reason unnaturally. Still frowning, they bared their teeth wide. This was supposed to be a smile. They looked like the Werewolf Man when he espies the Sleeping Beauty through the casement window.

Herb hopefully put his face down into the camera. The boy furtively elbowed the girl. She jabbed him back. Aunt Bett, yawning, stumbled back into the tree; someone hoisted her upright.

Just as Herb reached for the shutter button . . .

"This isn't right!" Stella Frobisher announced. "We should be *doing* something — something informal, like the instruction book says. See — I'm looking at an ornament."

She reached up high, touching a gilded glass ball. Promptly all of them — the whole twelve — turned and reached toward the same ornament. Even Rover the dog looked up. He thought it was something to eat.

"No, no," Herb cried out as he flashed a picture anyway. "Everybody be doing something *different.*"

This was worse. All tried to comply: Stella pointed fixedly at the ornament. Little Cheryl started doing the Charleston. Aunt Bett, always a game sport, demonstrated how she could do the trick of patting her head with one hand and simultaneously rubbing her stomach in circles with the other. Uncle Bart turned around, bent over and tried to touch his toes with his fingers.

"No, no, no! Don't move!"

The tension happily was broken as Rover, who seemed to be laughing at Herb, bounded in and around the room with the cat gambolling behind, standing on her hind legs and batting at his tail.

"There!" Uncle Bart shouted gladly. "Take a movie of *that!*"

It was no use, Herb realized, to explain he had a color-slide camera. He put it away, got out the movie camera, turned on the glare lights.

Immediately everybody froze stock-still.

Herb looked around for the dog and cat. They had both gone to sleep on the carpet, with their backs turned to him. They knew about the conspiracy too.

"All right, now!" Herb shouted buoyantly at the people. "Everybody be doing something!"

But they had taken his last admonition to heart. They stood at attention, staring back wide-eyed, transfixed, as if he were pointing a ray gun at them.

"Move, move, *move!*" he roared.

The only result was that Uncle Bart, anxious to be accommodating, started jiggling from one foot to the other. This made it look like an assemblage of wax dummies, one of which wanted to be excused.

Bill Bartley, another neighbor, agrees that people — and pets — have an unerring knack of knowing what will give a photographer a nervous breakdown.

"You can't tell *me* animals can't count," he insists. "Last Christmas I took a whole movie roll of the cat's tail twitching — I couldn't rouse her even by waving hamburger in my other hand. The moment I said aloud, 'That's the end of the last twenty-five feet,' the cat jumped up and went over to her dish, the canary flew out of her cage and ate beside the cat, my grandfather surprised us all by waking up and playing the fiddle and dancing a hornpipe. And our landlord, Old Man Scrooge himself, came knocking at the door dressed as Santa Claus."

The whole trick, of course, is to catch your subjects off guard — to capture that delightful natural atmosphere that goes with unposed photos. This deprives them of the chance to thwart you.

Sam McCool is a master of this art.

Sam's best informal scene was last Christmas season, when he got the inspiration of taking a surprise picture of the family watching TV after dinner. It *was* a surprise. In the semi-darkness, no one noticed him aiming the camera — they were too absorbed in the drama of the Mad Sniper drawing a bead on the heroine from a rooftop.

Suddenly the flashbulb went off. Everyone screamed. Sam would have had the most spectacular impromptu shot of the year — his mother-in-law upended on the floor behind the hassock, her legs pointing skyward — if he'd had another bulb.

"So I bought half a dozen *this* Christmas," he told me. "But can you beat it? She's not coming."

That's the exasperating thing about picture-taking. People will go to any lengths just to frustrate you.

But fortunately, good luck often strikes an amateur photographer like lightning. Even bad luck can prove to be a boon in disguise.

For instance: I made the beginner's mistake of forgetting that the roll of film in my movie camera had already been "taken"; I thought it hadn't.

I was filming a wedding reception on the grounds of a residential hotel. It's amazing, looking back now, to realize that in my unwitting eagerness to ruin a perfectly good completed roll, I re-took one side of it and then went to great trouble to find a dark room in the hotel to turn it over without getting the film light-struck.

There were no dark rooms. There never are.

In desperation I made my way up to the second floor and, in a narrow dim hallway, got down on my knees and huddled over the camera with my forehead touching the floor, to keep out the light while my fingers groped with the roll.

Old lady boarders stopped and stared.

"Poor man," commented one sympathetically. "He's got a cramp."

"Go 'way," I gritted through clenched teeth, my fingers working frantically to keep the film from slipping off the rollers. "Please go 'way."

"He's rubbing his stomach," one old lady told another. "He's telling the pain to go away."

More old ladies gathered. One started patting my back and told me it would be all right.

Clutching the loose camera case to my chest, still bent over, I fled down the stairs and asked a housemaid if there was a washroom handy.

She looked alarmed. She showed me into one by the kitchen. I rushed in gratefully, pushed the door almost shut with my foot to allow in only a glimmering of light. I started to open the camera again.

Unexpectedly a bare arm came through the doorway crack and snapped on a bright light.

"So you can see what you're doing, sir," said the maid's helpful voice outside. She closed the door.

I snapped the light off again with my elbow, finished turning the roll in the darkness by touch.

It was a shock to learn afterward the film was double-exposed. But if I do say it myself, I did a wonderful job of it.

The movie showed a salmon-angling friend of mine, stripped to the waist, standing in the Miramichi River unconcernedly scrubbing his chest — in the midst of ladies at a wedding reception in their pastel gowns. As the camera panned among the wedding guests on the lawn, my friend travelled with it, washing vigorously, as if he wasn't going to stop a good bath merely because they were in the river too.

Once he seemed to reach out and scrub fat old Miss Belham — he was really shaking water out of the brush — and she didn't seem to mind at all.

My elder son, an usher at the wedding, came into view from one side all dressed up, walked across the picture, immediately re-entered from the other side with a battered felt hat pulled down over his ears, his rubber boots on, a salmon rod over his shoulder, obviously saying the heck with all the formality, he was going fishing.

Next I appeared, unshaven, reeling in a good-sized trout on the lawn, right under the rector's nose. No amateur movies I have seen, or even professional ones, have duplicated this feat.

That's the marvel of home movies. You never know what your mistakes will do for you. More people ask to see that fishing trip on the lawn than any other reel I own.

And there's my very best color slide: Edinburgh Castle, taken from Princes Street one day while using a defective light meter. The picture is terrible — over-exposed, washed out, so faint you can barely see the ghostly outline of the distant castle.

"Say — wonderful!" people exclaim animatedly, "Edinburgh Castle in the Scottish morning mist — a real art photo! What time of the morning was it? What aperture, what stop, did you use?

I never answer, because I haven't the foggiest idea.

And of course there's Herb Frobisher's slide of the Christmas family gathering, with everyone pointing at the ten-cent Japanese ornament.

"*Bee-u-ti-ful!*" visitors cry admiringly. "What a meaningful idea — everybody looking up at the 'Star Shining Bright!' And the dog too — how did you ever get him to do it?"

"It was really nothing," says Herb. He's right.

As you can see, you have to be either brilliant or stupid to get remarkable home pictures.

It's no wonder all my friends can show you hundreds of remarkable ones — and will, if you don't get out in time.

I'm All Wrapped Up
for Christmas

On Christmas morning a million Canadian husbands, eyes alight with anticipation, will say, "Here are your presents, dear," and add with a slight touch of pardonable pride, "I did them up myself."

They will be stunned by what happens.

Instead of clasping delighted hands, a million wives will let out peals of laughter and double up helplessly, groping for a chair to collapse into.

The family, alarmed, will come running to Mother's side.

"Look!" she will finally gasp, amid fits of uncontrollable mirth, pointing, "Look how your father wrapped the presents!" And she will fold up again.

Daddy will manage to smile wanly, but he won't feel good at all.

"Wouldn't you know?" cries his older daughter. "He's got the bow on one side and the gift card on the other!"

"And dig *this* one!" exclaims an observant son. "You can read right through the tissue paper — 'Rodeo King Razor Blades'. Do you mean to say you're giving Mum *razor blades*?"

It is too late for Dad to explain how in the middle of the night he could find only one spare box to fit the white doe-skin gloves and understandably, in the rush, forgot to cover up the label with Christmas seals.

He's had it. He has been re-confirmed in his family's mind as a nut, a nincompoop, an incompetent, a hopeless bungler.

Why do wives do this?

It's an unconscious urge, I am convinced, to bring their husbands down a peg, to make them feel subservient and useless.

In this aim the salesgirls — the ones who sell Christmas wrappings to men — are the wives' willing allies.

I have noticed it repeatedly.

"Here you are, sir. Merry Christmas!" says the girl clerk, handing me my parcel. But she's smiling at me. I know what she's thinking.

No sooner do I begin tying up a box of crystal glasses when her strategy reveals itself. When I get the red ribbon all wound around, after turning the box over and over, I find I am tying the bow on the bottom side.

I'm no fool, of course. I know what will happen when the gift is unwrapped. The top will fall; the glasses will crash; and what will happen? Everyone will blame me.

So I try again — carefully. The box ends up the same way!

The answer is obvious.

The girl has sold me upside-down wrapping paper.

When I somehow manage to get the box right-end up and start to tie a pompom bow — you know, the pretty multiple kind that women love — her diabolical ingenuity shows up again.

Every time I tighten the ribbons of the second bow, the first bow gets smaller. When I tie the third bow, the second bow gets smaller; and the first bow becomes a knot.

At 3 A.M., by sheer perseverance — victory! Perhaps the final result does not look like a pompom, exactly. It looks like a kite tail. But the knots are all the same size.

You can see by this time what happened:

The girl sold me slippery ribbon.

If you don't believe it, listen to my friend Herb Frobisher.

Poor Herb — he is a victim of a common illusion. He always ties up his wife's presents himself, instead of getting the girls in the office to do it or letting the store gift-wrap them.

"Every husband," he confided to me happily, "has a sixth sense that tells him his wife will appreciate his own handiwork best. It means as much as the gift!"

So he bought the gaudiest gift wrapping he could find —

real shiny stuff with angels on it — and, in another store, seals and ribbon.

Incredibly, those two girls, in different stores, got together, their goal being to cross him up!

It became apparent the moment he started to tie the ribbon around all the corners of the electric-mixer carton — in that attractive diagonal way he had seen his wife do up gifts.

Herb is pretty smart. He held the ribbon down on the first corner with his stomach, the second corner with his elbow, and, laboriously, the third with his nose. But when he pulled the ribbon tight on the fourth corner, the whole business came off!

No matter how often he tried, he finished with the ribbon in his hands and an ache in his stomach, elbow and nose.

He had got slippery ribbon too!

After Herb eventually succeeded in tying the package straight-around, like a grocery package of sugar, he put the smiling Santa Claus stickers on.

Slowly the Santa Clauses curled up. The stickers refused to stick.

Herb found himself grabbing at popping Santas all over the box.

Naturally (it was now 4 A.M.) an exhausted husband can get pretty annoyed at this mischievousness.

"Lie down, you crumb!" he gritted at one cheerful Santa, slapping him back down. Santa, smilingly, did a slow push-up.

"LIE DOWN, BLAST YOU!" — despairingly.

From somewhere upstairs came Stella Frobisher's mystified voice:

"Herb! Who are you telling to lie down?"

She started down the stairs in her dressing gown. "Herb" — incredulously — "did you get the boys a *dog*?"

Wildly he ran out into the hall, waving his arms at her.

"Go back, for heaven's sake, go back! Good grief, can't a man wrap his Christmas presents without everybody spying on him? Go back! Go to bed! Lie down!"

She retreated, shaken. Upstairs her voice, with a plaintive

quaver to it, seemed to be saying over and over to herself "... not fair. If there's a pup down there, I should be told. It'll ruin the carpet!"

Fiercely Herb ran to the kitchen and made paste out of flour and water.

It wouldn't make the stickers stick.

In desperation he squeezed out a tube of airplane-model cement. They stuck!

To make doubly sure, he put the parcel face down on a dining room chair and piled books on it for weight.

At Christmas dawning, Herb cleverly sneaked down and removed the books.

It was a surprise for Stella, all right.

Wonderingly she descended the stairs with the kids, looking for the dog or wet spots.

"*Here's* your present," Herb said, pointing.

First she laughed at the wrapping, of course; then lifted the box. It was extraordinarily heavy — the chair came up too.

This seemed to upset her — especially as, when she shook the load, the chair fell away but the needlepoint seat remained attached to the carton.

"Mice!" she cried, terrified. "There're mice in our flour. It's all over the floor!"

It was perhaps only to be expected if, in the confusion, Herb gave his father-in-law a carefully wrapped box that turned out to be a pair of red woollen snuggies. Also, if his dear old mother-in-law, at the same moment, gaped to discover that Herb's gift for her this year was a brown carton labeled "Shepherd Boy Light Lager — 24 tins."

Perhaps the saddest instance of all, though, was that of Bill Bartley.

He allowed himself just thirty minutes on his Christmas Eve schedule to wrap up all the family gifts, having seen his wife Hilda easily finish hers in that time.

Of course, Bill had not counted on the perversity of the materials the girl sold him.

At 5 A.M. he was still struggling to coax the obstinate gilt-holly paper around a goosenecked lamp he had bought

Hilda — a lamp which, if she had no other use for it, would be just right for his den.

With the efficient, business-like approach that comes naturally to a man, Bill first set the lamp on one sheet of paper, and balanced another sheet on top of the shade. Then quickly, to take the wrappings by surprise, he folded the edges to make them meet. They stubbornly stayed apart.

Every husband will understand how this irked Bill, as it was not his fault. The girl had certainly sold him short wrapping paper.

He tried pulling the edges together by brute force, pushing the contrary lamp down by the neck, as it deserved, and fastening the sheets with safety pins. Now, unfortunately it looked like a bandaged volunteer in a Red Cross first-aid class.

Undaunted, Bill stuck several sheets of Christmas bells paper together, end to end, with electric tape from the garage; then wound them around and around the lamp, overlapping, from the bottom to the top. At least, thank goodness, it did not look like a half-alive first-aid patient any more. It looked dead. It looked like a mummified swan.

Bill, to his credit, is a decisive man. He will stand just so much nonsense from a goose-necked lamp.

At 6 A.M. he took the only sensible course. He hurled the wrinkled wrappings into the fireplace and marched the miserable thing upstairs and put it on his den desk.

But Bill, a generous soul, had one more present for Hilda — a long- and short-wave transistor radio kit — the kind you put together yourself.

He had taken quite an interest in this hobby lately, and thought it would be nice for Hilda if the house had a set.

In fact, at 7 A.M. he had it all over the living-room lounge chair, experimentally putting parts together.

By 7.30 — he could hear the kids stirring down the hall — Bill realized he was too bleary to complete the assembly in time. Pieces were still everywhere.

A resourceful inspiration struck him.

He threw a white sheet over the lounge to hide the surprise, and tied a red ribbon around the whole chair.

When Hilda came down, she laughed loud and long at how Bill had tied up her present — "just like a man, all thumbs."

Then Bill proudly lifted the sheet. Hilda stared. She had thought it was a new chair.

"It'll have to be put together, of course," he beamed. "You'll love it."

Suddenly she squealed.

"Oh, Bill, you're wonderful, *wonderful!*"

She hugged him tight. "Just what I've wanted for years! A stereo hi-fi!"

And she dashed for the phone and ecstatically told her mother.

Which is how it happened that two days after Christmas, Bill Bartley quietly had a mahogany stereo set delivered to the house.

It shows how smart husbands really are.

Or, maybe, how smart wives really are.

Thanks for the Lovely Christmas Present

(If Penned In A Moment Of Truthfulness)

Dear Aunt Meribel:

Agnes and I want to thank you for the beautiful large seashell. We put it on the table to look at whenever we wish we were at the seashore. We can't think of anything else to do with it, the novelty of taking turns holding it to our ear to "listen to the waves" having worn off by Christmas afternoon.

We remember that you often complained, when we were visiting you two years ago, what a dust-catcher the seashell was and if you ever had a bridge party you were going to get rid of it as a prize. We are sorry to see you never got around to having a bridge party. But we are going to have one very shortly, we can promise you that. And your present from us next Christmas is going to be quite a bit cheaper than this year.

Dear Cousin Judy:

We hadn't heard you were taking up woodcraft for a hobby, so Agnes and I were greatly surprised when we opened the present and found a tray made out of 4,000 match-sticks glued together, instead of the lovely cut-glass you usually send. You have no idea how often we use that cleverly-made tray; and it's a good thing you don't. We would prefer next year, if you must send matches, that you send them with the tops left on, in the original boxes.

Dear Uncle Bart:

It seems utterly impossible for an old goat like you to grasp the fact I kept growing after you left for the West. For twelve years now I have listened to Agnes' jibes every time I unwrap your parcel and find the Boys' Own Annual. As I

72

have no sons, only three daughters, could you at least switch to the Girls' Own Annual?

Dear Aunt Cissie:

I herewith acknowledge receipt of the letter that comes early each December stating you have been under heavy expense this year and therefore are sending only small gifts. As they have always been small, it is not necessary to keep on apologizing. We were interested to hear, in the same letter, how nice your new mink coat looks. Life must be very hard with unforeseen necessities always cropping up.

Dear Cousin John:

The girls were delighted with the plastic dolls you sent them. They were a little puzzled by the transparent tape on the elbows and knees until I explained that these were "hospital dolls," suitably bandaged. I refrained from telling them that the store-keeper you bought the dolls from had evidently used Scotch tape to patch the limbs after thoughtlessly letting his small daughters play with them. By the way, how did your little girls enjoy the Christmas season?

Dear Aunt Pam:

In the rush of Christmas mailing you neglected to rub out completely the price on the bottom of the box of pearls you sent Agnes, and we couldn't help noticing they cost $5.98. Strange to say, the "$5" was written with a soft-lead pencil and the ".98" with a hard-lead pencil. Do you suppose the store clerk changed pencils in the middle of writing the figure? For an example of how people should be more careful in this respect, look at the realistic "$6." in the "$6.79" on the box containing the antique brooch we sent you.

Dear Cousin Agatha:

Knowing how addle-pated you are, we were not surprised to discover you had sent us back the bread basket we sent you last year, with the addition of some crumbs wedged in the base. Don't bother to get agitated and ask us to send it back. It is coming back next Christmas, with fresh crumbs.

73

Dear Great-Aunt Prue:

We were both so sure you would send a better present this year, after coming into Great-Uncle Will's money in September, that we made the mistake of mailing you a whole set of six high-neck lace collars instead of the usual one. When we found a hankie for each of us in your Christmas card, Agnes said, "The old devil will probably die with every cent untouched." I think that Agnes for the first time is probably right. Please return five of the collars.

Dear Sister-in-law Kate:

It was very original, even for a trouble-maker like you, to think of sending the children a box of fireworks for Christmas. They opened them before Agnes and I were awake — and when they lit that lawn flare under the tree I understand it was really something to see. The Hendersons were kind enough to take us in for Christmas dinner, and the Salvation Army has just been here to distribute clothing. The insurance adjustor is urging us to enter a claim against you, but I said no, we want to stay on good terms with you until next Christmas, as I have an original little present to send you. Disregard any ticking you may hear as you unwrap the present, as it is all part of the surprise.

Men Vs.
Women

Women
Are Crazy
About Money

When the news came out that women now control 80 per cent of the buying power of Canada, it was the last straw for my bachelor friend Wes Brewley.

"Something should be done!" he exploded. "They don't know how to handle money."

You had to give Wes credit. He really meant it. He had battled for years with heroic determination to keep women in their place.

Wes Brewley was the final guard-rock to be knocked out when the wives crumpled the defences of the Highland Curling Club. He fought to the last desperate dumbbell to keep them out of the local YMCA. He cast a futile anti-social vote to bar them from the City Social Club. In short, he was the original anti-Women's Lib partisan guerilla.

If he knew he was waging a hopeless rearguard action, he never admitted it. That was a measure of the man's wonderful character.

Now, impulsively, he launched his greatest campaign. He started a one-man survey to prove the feminine sex was helplessly irresponsible in financial matters.

I'm glad to say he got amazing results.

He found old Bob Treadwell, a retired banker, at the Atlantic Salmon fly-tying club and asked him point-blank: "Did you run into many amusing experiences with women customers at the bank? Aren't you worried about them taking over the spending power of the nation?"

Bob Treadwell, meticulously fixing a crimson shoulder feather from a red-winged blackbird on top of a golden pheasant crest, answered slowly:

"Oh, banking has its lighter side all right! When I was working in Hamilton a fellow came in every year and paid his income tax with a check written out on his shirt cuff to the Receiver-General of Canada. He pinned a note to it: 'You've got everything else — you might as well take my shirt.' " Old Bob laughed uproariously at his own recollection.

Another retired banker, Will Hanneman, holding a wisp of Asiatic blue kingfisher in one hand and scarlet dyed rabbit fur in the other, joined in the guffaws, adding:

"It's perfectly legal, you know. You can write a check on a beer label if you wish. Why, I've seen a trapper write one on birch bark. Or you can write one on an egg — there's a check that can't bounce, ha, ha!"

Reluctantly Wes Brewley interrupted their mirth.

"But what about *women* customers? What crazy things did they do?"

Both men pondered in their armchairs, uncomfortably.

"It's devilish hard when you ask quick-like," said old Bob Treadwell.

"That's it," sighed Will Hanneman. "Devilish hard."

"Were there women," my friend pressed eagerly, "who thought a bank draft was something you catch cold from? Or a posting machine was to mail letters? Or a penny roll was a bun? Or who always wanted clean fresh germ-free bills?"

"No-o-o," replied Bob Treadwell thoughtfully, "most wanted ordinary used bills. They complained the brand-new ones stuck together in their purse."

"They do, too," agreed Will Hanneman.

"But," Wes Brewley persisted, "what about the *silly* women, the ridiculous ones? You know — the average women customers. Weren't there any who wanted to deposit money but didn't want the teller to know how much, because it was no one's business but their own?"

Bob Treadwell reflected a moment, then brightened.

"Yes, we had secretive customers . . . The worst were the coin collectors — awful! Of course, they were men, always peering down furtively at their change, or staring over the shoulder of the man ahead in line to see what he got. They could hardly get to the front door before they opened their penny rolls and sneaked a look."

"Addicts," agreed Will Hanneman. "Compulsive addicts."

My friend was growing impatient. Every man knew that women were naive about handling money. You gave a woman a cheque book and she thought she could write cheques. These bankers couldn't seem to remember.

"Aren't women absurdly superstitious?" he asked hopefully. "Don't they sometimes want all their change in silver dollars or something?"

"Ah!" cried Bob Treadwell, admiring a bright blue-dyed grizzly hackle held in his fingers. "*Now* you've hit on something! When I worked in Cape Breton, I couldn't keep up with the demand for fifty-cent pieces. We never had enough."

"The women didn't trust dollar bills?"

"It was the fish buyers who asked for them," he replied. "They wanted them for the fishermen — I never found out why. It's funny about preferences. Canadians aren't the only odd people. New York bankers find themselves clogged with half-dollars, pennies accumulate in Pittsburgh and Dallas, nickels and dimes in Louisville, Nashville and Baltimore."

"And two-dollar bills!" interjected Will Hanneman helpfully. "When I was in Chester, Nova Scotia, in the thirties you couldn't get an American tourist to take a two-dollar bill — he'd push it right back at you. For a while the U.S. stopped making them. No one wanted them."

Wes Brewley thanked them, and left them to their ostrich and jungle cock feathers. You see? — his campaign had already proved one point. It had proved that old bankers were out of touch with reality.

On a happy inspiration he asked somebody who'd know — his own bank manager.

"I remember well," reminisced the manager, Mr. Trentham, shaking his head, "when the scarcity of men in World War II compelled the banks to put women in the cages. I was opposed to it."

"And when," Wes Brewley asked sympathetically, "do you think you'll be able to get men again?"

Mr. Trentham looked at him aghast.

"Never, I hope! The girls are faster, quicker with their hands. They can count out bills and take part in repartee and then turn away. A male teller on his way to a manager's job is apt to hold things up by examining a cheque and saying to himself, 'Now, why would they pay him that much?' And men customers don't delay girl tellers by asking them for business advice — they go to the assistant manager with a touch of gray at his temples."

He was speaking expansively, sitting back with fingers interlaced across his vest, noting with satisfaction the customer lineups before the wickets manned by girl tellers outside his office.

Wes Brewley was never one to be discouraged easily. He had his big question ready:

"But don't girl tellers create embarrassing situations sometimes in handling money?"

"Indeed they do," agreed Mr. Trentham, smiling. Wes Brewley perked up.

"Talk about embarrassment!" mused the manager. "It's a laugh to see the men customers jockeying to stay in line for their favorite pretty tellers — the ones they give chocolates to at Christmas — and trying to pretend they don't hear when another girl teller calls out, 'Could I serve you, sir?' And do the men ever look awkward sometimes — you know how easily men get flustered — when they pick up their change and forget their bills, or when they absently put the bank pen into their inside coat pocket and start away and get yanked back by the chain."

Chuckling, he went on, "The same girl teller caught old man Coggins three times this week!"

Wes Brewley — who for years had been going to the lone male teller left in the bank — was appalled to hear what women were doing to banking.

"*Think*," he pleaded. "Can't you even remember one time that a woman customer did something foolish?"

Mr. Trentham pondered, then acknowledged frankly:

"Yes ... I can. It was back about thirty years ago, when the income tax notice of a coming refund looked very much like a cheque. There was this woman, a widow ..."

"She knew nothing about money?"

"That was the trouble — she did. She always knew her exact balance. Oh, like a good many widows left in their fifties, she knew nothing at first — they've all been brainwashed by their husbands and told that handling money was beyond them — but when she found herself on her own, she learned fast. So when this lady brought in a refund advance notice for $17.85, the teller promptly cashed it for her."

"A girl teller?" — hopefully.

Mr. Trentham hung his head.

"I was the teller. But you see, she was always so precise I relied on her implicitly."

Poor Wes Brewley. To compound his disappointment, he discovered the very next day the male teller was gone. In his place was Miss McKintrock, a honey blonde whom the manager regarded as the best teller in the bank.

Wes had no choice but to go to her. A last desperate thought occurred to him: Perhaps she would do something so outrageously woman-like, it would prove the very point he was trying to make.

Like many bachelors, Wes was a methodical man. He had planned his early lunch-hour like a military operation. In his pocket was an envelope of silver coins his nephew had saved up; Wes was going to make up the difference and open a $5 bank account for him. Estimated time needed: four minutes. Then he would walk to the Hydro office to pay his light bill. Time: eleven minutes. And then to the City Welfare Sewing Centre to give them a collection of fancy old buttons that belonged to his aunt. Time: fourteen minutes.

"Good morning!" said Miss McKintrock liltingly; and Wes Brewley was struck by the happy genuineness of her smile. "What can I do for you today?"

He watched, unaccountably flustered, for her to do something ridiculous.

"I'd — I'd like to open an account for my nephew," he mumbled, stern-visaged.

"My, isn't that a nice thing to do!" — her blue eyes were surprisingly dazzling, up close — "I didn't realize you had a nephew."

"Oh, yes!" Wes heard his voice saying. "He's a boy." He had meant to say: "He's only young."

"That's lovely," said Miss McKintrock, still smiling. Wes

80

was amazed to think that in such a coldly commercial place anyone could be always so marvelously natural and pleasant.

"I ... I ..." — he hurriedly fumbled in his pockets — "I would like to bank this much for him."

On the counter, with a clatter that seemed to fill the bank, he poured from an envelope a cascade of buttons — pearl buttons, wooden buttons shaped like crosses, gold-tinted buttons, sea-shell buttons.

The hum of conversation in the bank ceased.

Dumbstruck, his ears burning, Wes Brewley waited to be laughed out of the place.

Miss McKintrock was laughing — but not at him, at the incredible variety of the buttons.

"Thank *goodness*," she exclaimed, "for someone with an original sense of humor ... aren't they simply beautiful!"

"Are they?" he gasped, staring blankly.

"*Gorgeous* ... look at this one — an oval bone button with darling crochet work all around it! Wouldn't it make a lovely pendant?"

"Take it," Wes gulped. "Take them all!"

"No, no ... but could I really have this one?"

"All of them!" Wes heard his voice blurting in relief. "I've got plenty — I'll bring lots more tomorrow ... "

Which was why, when Mr. Trentham glanced out of his office that afternoon, he sat back happily and twiddled his fingers on his vest as he watched a red-faced Wes Brewley maneuvering around with a paper bag in his hands, trying to get in the right lineup and self-consciously ignoring the voice from the next empty wicket, "Could I serve you, sir?"

Mr. Trentham almost laughed out loud when Wes, on leaving Miss McKintrock's wicket, put the bank pen in his pocket and got yanked back.

But Mr. Trentham won't twiddle delightedly much longer — because that was five weeks ago, and I heard just today Miss McKintrock is getting married next month.

It happened to be Wes Brewley who told me, and he is putting her name in already for membership in the Highland Curling Club, the YMCA Ladies' Association and the City Social Club.

The Importance of
Being Somebody

"To maintain his self-respect it is essential for a man to feel he *is* somebody in his own home." — Prof. Desmond Winter, British psychologist, in a news interview.

That's exactly right. I know I'm full of self-respect, because I'm certainly somebody in my house.

Why, early this evening my wife came home from shopping and said, "Somebody had better bring the groceries in from the car if anybody expects dinner in time to get out and play cards tonight." I knew right off whom she meant. I ran and lugged in all the cartons so I could be sure of getting out in time.

No sooner had we finished the dishes than she said, "Somebody's going to get an awful surprise if I find any more clothes dropped around the house." I knew who this was, too. I picked up my hat and coat from the coffee table and hung them up — even though I was going to put them on in half a minute.

When I turned around, I was surprised to see she was holding some sponges and a can of gummy substance in her hands. "If somebody doesn't help me clean down these walls," she said, "they needn't expect me to lend them any money."

As I was just about to mention this very subject to her — the money, not the walls — I realized suddenly I wasn't in such a hurry as I thought. I grabbed a handful of wallpaper cleaner and went to work.

Later when I put on my newly dry-cleaned hat in front of the mirror, my wife commented, "You think you're somebody, don't you?"

I don't know why she asked me that, because she should know: If there's anybody in my house who's somebody, it's me.

82

Women Leave Me
Speechless

Everybody is taking a personality-development course these days — like the one described in this leaflet: "Learn to hold your chin up. . . . Shake hands firmly. . . . Look your fellow man in the eye. . . . Speak convincingly. . . . Impress your friends!"

I haven't taken the course. My chin seems to hold up all right. I can shake a man's hand firmly to impress him, and look him straight in the eye; and, if he has taken a course, he will shake my hand even more firmly and look me straighter in the eye to impress *me*. This compels us to keep standing there like two roosters meeting for the first time until a mutual friend hurriedly breaks it up under the impression we are about to fight.

So much for my fellow men.

What *I* need — what I hope someone will invent soon — is a short course in how to meet my fellow women.

I can't speak to women. I can't say anything to them properly.

Like the other evening when my wife was having a bridge game, and Mr. Breetham dropped off his portly wife at the door.

I wasn't sure at first, as the car drove up, that it *was* Mrs. Breetham, because he often drives around with his St. Bernard sitting in the front seat, and silhouettes are deceiving.

"Well, well, Mrs. Breetham!" I said jocularly as she puffed up the steps. "I wasn't sure whether it was you or Flop-Ears."

By her face I could tell she didn't see the joke of it. A man would have laughed. Mrs. Breetham didn't laugh.

"Thank you," she said, with a strange tight-lipped smile, and swept past me. This gave me a guilty feeling.

I tried to make up for it a minute later, when I saw her

looking at herself in the hall mirror before going into the living room.

"My, my," she exclaimed self-deprecatingly, half to herself. "I completely forgot to put on my foundation cream — I look so much homelier than I did yesterday."

She paused, waiting for me to reassure her. I did. I hastened to say, "Oh, I'm sure you don't."

Mrs. Breetham glanced at me coldly.

"You're sure I'm not any homelier than I was yesterday? Thank you." And with a superior smile she flounced into the living room.

I realized she had me jinxed. I couldn't say anything right to her. I racked my mind to think of a compliment that would mollify her feelings.

Her sponge cake — that was it! I remembered the wonderful sponge cake she served the last time we were at her house. It was beautiful — light, fluffy, buoyant, springy, full of nice air bubbles, not soggy like some people make. I frantically searched for a word to describe its texture. An inspiration hit me as she walked out to the telephone.

"Oh, Mrs. Breetham," I said cheerily, "I'll always remember your sponge cake. It was just like sponge rubber!"

It didn't mollify her. "Thank you again," she said, and left me standing there baffled.

When, after the party, my wife begged Mrs. Breetham not to bother calling a taxi — that I would gladly drive her — and Mrs. Breetham protested airily, I saw a chance to redeem myself.

I intended to say:

"Oh, yes, I always *love* to drive you home."

But it came out:

"Oh, yes, I always love to drive you *home*."

"Well," said Mrs. Breetham with an acid smile. "It's nice to be frank."

You see? I only gave her a chance to bat me down again.

That's the trouble I find about talking to women. They misinterpret what I say. They twist me all up. They leave me tongue-tied. They take a diabolical delight in embarrassing me. They love to make a man feel foolish.

84

It's easy to greet a man on the street. You can just mumble "Day" (for Good Day) or "Do" (for How Do You Do) without disturbing your train of thought. But that's too curt for women. You have to think what to say. They expect something fancy, like "Isn't it a lovely day?" — in which case you have to look around quick to see if it is — or a compliment, like "You look very nice today."

The drawback is, with me, it always comes out: "You look very nice *today*."

So I try not to say such things at all. I try to say something that fits the acquaintance. Like a woman I know who's crazy about cats and always telling anecdotes about their cleverness. When I met her the other day, to remind her of her favorite subject, I said:

"Well, well, Mrs. Holscomb! Whenever I see you I think of a cat."

She took me up on it immediately. Her pupils dilated. Her ears flattened. She pounced on me like a helpless mouse:

"Thank *you* very much."

I stammered. I gulped. I tried to explain. She wouldn't listen. She was pretending she was insulted, and she loved it. She enjoyed seeing me writhe.

"That will be all right," she said with mock aloofness, brushing past me. "My feelings aren't easily hurt."

One of my worst troubles is finding myself in conversation with a woman whose name I should know but can't remember. If it was a man I could greet him with, "Well, you old rooster, where've you been lately?" and he'd tell me everything about himself, including his name.

But you can't call a woman an old hen, nor, unfortunately, an old lobster, an old blister, an old walrus or an old goat.

I found myself sitting next to an attractive young woman in a restaurant last week. I hadn't seen her for years. I knew her maiden name — Miss Healy — but I had no idea what her married name was. To seek a clue I ventured casually:

"Er — how many children do you have now?"

She smiled sweetly.

"I'm not even married."

I swallowed hard. I could feel the crimson creeping up

85

my neck. I had to get out of it quick. So, trying to explain gallantly that she looked so pretty I was certain that some man must have snapped her up, I blurted:

"Oh, sorry! I just thought you looked as if you *should* be married."

This didn't seem to help.

So you see, the harder I've tried to speak graciously to women, the worse it's turned out. I don't know why.

There was Mrs. Bollett, who called on us one evening when I had a headache. She carried on such a sprightly conversation that the headache disappeared. I told her gratefully next day, "You know, I felt a lot better after you left."

"*Thank* you," she said in a strange tone.

I enthusiastically told Mrs. McCooley, who wanted to paint landscapes but didn't think she could, "You should at least attempt it — why, talent is very often found where no one would expect to find any."

She thanked me peculiarly too.

When Dean Berrywell's wife, who is quite hefty, climbed out of his car backwards when they came to call, it occurred to me that lobsters often walk backwards. So I remarked lightly, "You looked just like a lobster getting out of that car."

She turned on me red-faced, which made her look all the more like a lobster. "Thank you," she said. I could see that somehow I had said the wrong thing.

"I didn't mean," I explained painfully, "that you look like a lobster; you just got out of the car like a lobster would."

This didn't seem to help. It sounded as if she crawled, waving her arms and antennae.

I hastened to explain further:

"Did you know that lobsters sometimes walk backwards?"

I realized with dismay that what I meant hadn't sunk in.

"There's no need to change the subject," she said haughtily. "I heard what you said the first time."

That's why I think a short course should be offered in how to talk with women. Even a little booklet like an English-Hindustani dictionary, containing forty phrases that can be spoken to women without arousing resentment, would be a great help.

And there are such phrases. I found one the other day. Women, I discovered, like you to notice their hair.

I went into the bank that day and, as always, tried to think of something pleasant to say to the lady teller that wouldn't make her thank me in that odd tone.

She was a very pretty girl, and she had her hair done up in a new coiffure — one of those things that my wife told me today is called an "upswept."

I walked right up to the counter and said to her brightly, "Well, well! I see you're wearing an uplift today."

She must have been flattered, because she blushed to the roots of her hair.

In fact, every time I've been in the bank since then she has blushed.

It just shows that you can sometimes say the right thing to a woman.

It's Not True
What They Say About
Women Back-Seat Drivers

As every husband will tell you, a wife sitting anywhere in a car is a menace to life and limb.

It's sheer foolhardiness, of course, to let her take the wheel. It is equally nerve-wracking, he will point out, to let her sit beside him when he's driving, because she will utter sudden shrieks about what she sees just ahead. And to let her sit in the back seat, where she can squeal warnings about things she can't see but thinks must be just ahead — that is the greatest hazard of all. A woman in the back seat will almost put a capable driver into the ditch every time.

I don't believe a word of it, myself. I have never heard of a back-seat wife who actually put her husband into the ditch; it's always, you will notice, *almost*. Bees sometimes do it, but not wives.

The truth of it is that the "woman back-seat driver menace" is just a legend. It is a product of men's resourceful imagination. Undoubtedly it originated with some husband back in the early 1900's who wanted an excuse to keep his wife out of the car. And as it is the sort of legend that appeals greatly to men, it has been carefully preserved and handed down from generation to generation, from father to son to grandson. Unfortunately, many a present-day husband has grown up believing it implicitly. Just let his wife climb into the back seat and his nerves will start going to pieces immediately, even if she isn't saying a word.

Let me cite an illustration:

A friend of mine took his wife and son and daughter to a home at Westfield, fourteen miles from town, where a young people's party was being held.

His wife, after the habit of wives, was in the back seat.

But all the way to Westfield the children were talking so animatedly about the party they were going to that she didn't have a chance to speak.

When the man stopped the car for the young folks to get out, he was anxious to get started again quickly. The car was in a dip in the highway and the rain was pouring down; the visibility was poor in case another car came along.

"Have a good time!" he called out to them as they hurried up the gravel path.

"Have a good time!" his wife echoed.

Then the driver stepped on the gas.

"Dirty night," he observed over his shoulder to his wife as the car roared over the rise and picked up speed on the straightaway.

She didn't say a word. And he knew why, too. He had been away fishing all that day, and wives are notoriously unable to understand why husbands sit for hours in a rowboat in the rain with no certainty of bringing anything home except a good cold or a hangover from what they take to prevent them from getting a cold.

"Anything special you'd like to hear on the radio?" he asked, switching it on.

Nothing but ominous silence in the back seat. This made him feel tense and nervous.

He held a package of cigarettes over his shoulder.

"Like a cigarette?"

Frozen silence.

Lamely he put the package back in his pocket and settled down to drive. If she was so determined not to talk, he wouldn't talk either. But he was feeling more wrought up every moment. That's what a sullen woman in the back seat can do to a man.

When he drove into the yard of his home, he turned around to back the car into the garage — and got the surprise of his life.

The back seat was empty.

He realized with a shock what had happened. She had got out, intending to move up front with him for the trip back to town.

He had left her standing in the downpour fourteen miles up the road.

The phone was ringing when he opened the front door.

It was Westfield calling. It was the man at whose house the party was being held. Said he casually, "Didn't you forget something?"

The husband groped for words. None came out.

"Never mind," said the cheery voice on the phone. "She's on her way to town in a taxi, so you have nothing to worry about."

That's what *he* thought.

When the wife strode into the house, her mouth firmly tensed, she didn't find the husband waiting up to be knocked down. He was already down — he was in bed, apparently fast asleep, though he was snoring extraordinarily loud.

This, I am sure, proves that a man *can* become a nervous wreck merely by imagining that his wife is in the back seat. It's not the wives who do it. It's the men themselves.

Have
a Happy
Holiday

How to Train
for Your Vacation

Do you always feel knocked out on vacation trips? Do you get tired, tense and trigger-tempered? Do you still see roads unwinding when you go to bed?

Of course you do; everybody does! That's how silly everybody is. Nobody gets properly into shape for the holiday season.

I'm an exception. I decided to be ready this year. As soon as the road maps began arriving I went into spring training. I didn't tell my wife because that would spoil the surprise of it. I wanted her to see how fresh and nimble I kept on the trip.

She was, I must say, surprised from the start. So were our neighbors the McGillises and the Stackpoles.

First I practised making quick stops at our corner when I was coming home from work. Those Boston traffic jams can be nerve-wracking if you're not prepared for them.

Time after time I pretended I saw a big furniture van looming up at the empty intersection and slammed down the brake so hard my head nearly bumped the windshield, then started again swiftly with a screech of tires.

When I got into the house my wife was furious.

"I've had calls from Amy Stackpole and Helen McGillis both," she said, "and they think it's disgraceful, at five o'clock in the afternoon, too."

I didn't tell her. I wanted her to be surprised.

Next morning when I started for the garage in the rain without my rubbers she was quite upset. She couldn't seem to grasp that I was preparing myself not to be annoyed by forgetting something on the trip — you know how you always forget a toothbrush or rubbers and it spoils the whole trip. She ran for the closet to get my rubbers.

"Thanks just the same," I said, "but I'm pretending I haven't any rubbers today," and I walked out. Going down the sidewalk I could see her peering at me from the kitchen window.

She didn't say very much that evening when I announced I wanted to sleep in a different bed — you know how strange mattresses will ache your back unless you're used to changes. So I slept in each of our kids' beds the next two nights, as they were away for the weekend. In fact, it was about then she stopped speaking to me. All she said when the children asked, "Who's been sleeping in *my* bed?" was, firm-lipped, "That's Goldilocks over there reading the paper."

Nor did she say much the next evening when I turned up the record player to make it play the crash of ocean breakers over and over all night — you know the record, the one with the seagulls mewing — so we'd be accustomed to the noise in case we got a cabin by the seashore. The only thing she said, when she woke up with a start at 3 A.M., was "Lord! I can't stand much more of living here!"

That encouraged me. It showed she wasn't in any shape to take a trip either.

Well, you've guessed it. My vacation training proved a great success.

The morning we were starting out — the morning after I brought home the three live mosquitoes and let them go in our bedroom (you know how a mosquito singing in a tourist cabin can upset your nerves if you're not used to them) — I woke up and found the family gone.

They had left without me.

I slept in my own bed for my holidays, had no mosquitoes, heard no breakers, got in no Boston traffic jams.

So if you're interested in a carefree vacation, kindly line up on the right and for the small sum of two dollars you can have my new Happy Holidays Training Kit, complete with informative leaflet, one phonograph record of ocean waves and seagulls (on the opposite side, truck horns honking and a New Year's Eve party in full progress) and three live mosquitoes.

Everything's
Up to Date in
Dear Old Blighty

My wife and I were talking about the problem of catching on to strange English ways.

At our London hotel my wife stepped into the tub after closing the bathroom door.

As she found herself sitting in semi-darkness, she pushed the switch button on the wall over the tub.

Nothing happened.

"This light is on the blink!" she called out to me in the bedroom. "Open the door a little!"

As I started over, a knock came on the bedroom door.

"Are you all right in there?" — the night porter's solicitous voice.

"Open the *door* a little!" — my wife's petulant voice.

"Yes! Yes!" Harassed, I was trying to answer both. Then, through the bathroom door to my wife: "Keep quiet! You're waking up the whole hotel!"

"Is someone in trouble in the bath?" — the porter again.

"NO!" I shouted, rattled, wondering how he knew. "It's only my wife."

"Then, sir" — imperturbably — "does your wife need assistance?"

"No; it's just the light switch isn't working."

"I can't *hear* you" — my wife's voice again — "Open the door a little!"

"I think you'll find, sir" — the polite voice from the corridor — "she's pressing the emergency alarm button. The light switch is outside the bathroom."

And so it was.

Like any wary North American couple in a strange city,

we made sure to lock our bedroom door before retiring. We didn't want any of those Skinheads breaking in.

So it was only natural, when my wife opened her eyes at dawn next morning and saw a strange man wearing a pill-box hat standing by her bed, she screamed "Eeeeeeeeek!"

I sprang to my feet in the adjoining bed, ready to grapple with the intruder.

"Your tea, sir," said the stranger, depositing a tray on the bedside table. He carefully placed a morning newspaper between my hairy bare feet as I stood in my bed and, apparently oblivious of the peculiar ways some North Americans wake up, quietly left.

A few days later we dropped in at a little country inn which had a sign "Cream Tea" in the window. I was excited. If there was cream for tea, there might be cream for coffee! I had never got adjusted to the English custom of coffee served with hot milk. ("Black or white?" the hotel waiter always asked, and if you said "White" he poured coffee and milk simultaneously, using both hands. Eventually you got the unconscious impression there must be no cream in England.)

We ordered "cream coffee" and, incredibly, the waitress brought scones, crumpets, butter, strawberry jam — and a huge bowl of Dorset cream so thick you could stand up a spoon in it. This I promptly did to the evident amazement of local English people at tables nearby.

Then I scooped up a gob and stirred it richly into my cup of coffee.

Suddenly I became aware that all conversation in the tearoom had stopped. Everyone was watching me.

So I stared back, wondering how English people could possibly put cream in their coffee any other way.

An elderly woman buttered her scone; then spread jam on the butter; then ladled thick cream on top of the jam — and poured hot milk in her coffee.

That's the trouble with Canadians. Unprepared, we cross the Atlantic expecting the English to follow Canadian customs, which we know of course are the most sensible in the world. But for some reason they don't; they insist on having their own. This startles us constantly.

95

For instance, when I got off the plane at London airport, I saw a woman standing amidst the crowds swirling past, holding aloft a sign. It said simply "J. Davey."

"Isn't that ingenious!" I remarked to an Englishman beside me. "She's looking for someone — probably her husband — and holding up the sign so Mr. Davey can't miss her. But how did she get it printed so nicely?"

"That," he said patiently, "is a car-hire firm. She's looking for customers."

So you can see, I guessed it right. She *was* looking for somebody. But I'm glad he told me. Later, after seeing different women all holding up the same sign at various English airports, I'd have wondered what J. Davey was up to.

I must confess I was almost caught off guard the next morning. After getting over the surprise of having tea in bed, I was standing in the middle of the bedroom floor surveying myself in the mirror before dressing. Being weight-conscious, I was appraising what kind of shape I was in.

Suddenly the door lock clicked and the maid walked in.

This is a traditional custom in English hotels. I can only assume all Englishmen dress in bathrooms.

Fortunately, I became so instantly aware of what was happening — in that split-second of the "click" — that by the time the door opened I had leaped right across the room and behind the dresser. That's quite a trick, to throw yourself in a curve. It showed at least I was in good shape physically.

But the very circumstance that an arising guest could leisurely assess his physique in the bedroom mirror in March belied the well-known truth that all English hotels are chilly.

It *must* be true, of course, because several Canadian friends who had not been to England since World War I assured me of it. Their opinion was backed up by several Canadians who had never been to England at all.

Yet I didn't find one hotel like that. It has worried me ever since.

Arriving in Oxford, I was shown by the luggage porter to the wrong room.

He turned the key, strode in. A dignified middle-aged Englishman was sitting comfortably in an armchair, his knees crossed, reading a book. He was not exactly stark naked, because he was wearing gold-trimmed spectacles.

I have to admire the English aplomb. Did *he* leap clear across the room? No; he didn't even put down the book. He only tilted his head slightly, to get us in the focus of his glasses. Then, when he had us, he said: "Yes?"

"Frightfully sorry," the porter said, backing out.,

Before I slammed the door in embarrassment, the gentleman had resumed reading. What I mean is, he certainly wasn't chilly.

This illustrates a facet of national behavior I noticed repeatedly: The English will go to any extremes to hide the shortcomings they're famous for, like drafty hotels.

Another widely-known fact is that the average Englishwoman is hearty, tweedy, outdoorsy, horsey, stodgy and flat-heeled. Haven't we all met her a hundred times in well-loved novels?

The English were diabolically artful in concealing the average woman from me. During five weeks in their country I never met her once. The females I saw looked glamorously beautiful, svelte, with a heart-stopping Continental flair. Chorus lines in London musical comedies were dazzling. Each girl was a young hand-picked lovely. Not one seemed to be the producer's cousin, like every fourth girl on Broadway.

I realized immediately I'd been taken in, because I've heard any number of Canadian businessmen who went over on those chartered trade-promotion flights assure their wives that English women were as the novels described them. You've undoubtedly heard the same thing, if you happened to be fortunate enough to meet any of these businessmen before they hurriedly arranged to go back the very next year to look into more business.

Everyone has always known for a fact, too, that Englishmen are coldly aloof. They insist this isn't so; but I found it out for myself on a train from Bournemouth to London. I sat at the same dining-car table as a man who remained frozen-faced silent for eighty miles. He was wearing a pink beret, which marked him as a typical individualistic Englishman. Several times I almost spoke to him, but thought better of it.

Finally I said: "Nice evening," and he spoke up slowly — this after eighty miles, mind you — "Yes."

I asked him what part of England he was from, and he said Sarnia, Ontario.

He asked me what part of the United States I was from, and I told him Saint John, New Brunswick.

That's all we said, as the train was about to arrive in London. It gives you a pretty good idea of how much communicativeness you can expect on English trains, no matter what the English say.

And it's common knowledge that the English are hopelessly old-fashioned. How can they deny it? Why, in London I saw dappled white-and-gray horses still hauling brewery vans — imagine! — while hordes of tourists vied to take pictures of them. Some tourists said they had stayed an extra day in London just to get good movies of those anachronistic dray horses. An Englishman informed me the same horses double as steeds to draw carriages in royal processions, and that North American tourists sometimes remain a whole week extra at their fancy London hotels to capture the sight on movie film. True, while I was spending some additional time in London myself to photograph the beer horses, I saw several stupendously giant air liners whistling overhead, and a plane that rose straight up and then shot forward like an arrow. It just shows *somebody* in England must be keeping up with the times.

Talk about old-fashioned: In my London hotel, when I asked the way to the barber shop, the porter said: "Would you like an appointment with the hairdresser, sir?" I realized he must be thinking I wanted an appointment for my wife, so I hastened to make it clear to him. He didn't seem to understand he had made an error; he just said, "A quarter to five, sir."

Well, when I arrived there on the second floor at a quarter to five, anxious to get another cheap English haircut before I went home, guess what I found? Three men with hairnets on, sitting in three chairs, and one chair empty!

I resolved they were not going to put any quaint hair-net on me.

The English barber cut my hair, lamenting continually that I was refusing to stay another two months so he could "shape" it properly — and then, before I knew it, I was wheeled forward and my head was dunked in the sink.

As my head went down, I glimpsed the barber drawing a hairnet out of a drawer.

A tall feminine assistant, a Continental girl with green eye-shadow on her upper lids, started expertly shampooing my head in the sink. I was convulsed by the thought of what my wife would say if she could see me with a hairnet on.

Suddenly the girl said concernedly: "Excuse me, sir, but are you all right?"

"Yes," I burbled, head in the suds.

"Well, why does your head shake so?"

"I'm" — gasp — "laughing."

"Oh? So? And why are you laughing?"

"I don't know." I didn't dare tell her.

"Oh" — puzzled — "So?" She was left thinking I always laughed when I got my head in a sink.

Then abruptly I was drawn upright; my hair was towelled, and combed; and a hairnet was clamped on. The girl brought an electric blower to dry it.

"Ah!" she said in a moment. "And now for the friction."

I begged off vociferously. I had an important visitor to keep an appointment with; I couldn't stay any longer.

"Cannot you wait for the friction?" The Continental girl sounded anxious. "No," I said in mild alarm. "I must go immediately."

"He cannot have the friction," the girl explained earnestly to the hairdresser. "He must go now."

The barber seemed distraught.

They reluctantly excused me, and charged me £2 ($5.20), which was somewhat different from the signs in the little barber shops downtown that said: "Beards trimmed, 3/6 . . . Haircut, 4s."

I didn't find out until I returned to Canada, and sur-reptitiously got my wife to ask a hairdresser friend what a "friction" might be, that it was probably an electric-vibrator massage treatment. Somehow it was a letdown.

I had great fun telling everyone about the picturesque old English barbering customs, until one day I read a news dispatch in our own paper:

PHILADELPHIA — An international barbers' convention was told today that the next advance in North American men's hair-cutting would be a comprehensive trim-shampoo-electric drying technique recently introduced in Europe, with the use of a hairnet. Total cost: $6.50.

That's the great difficulty about visiting England — trying to figure out what is old and obsolete and laughable and what is really so new you haven't heard about it yet.

But I think I proved that a really wide-awake Canadian can suavely cope with English customs without appearing to be surprised or discomfited at any time.

Take, for instance, my trip by car from London to Oxford. A green-uniformed government chauffeuress was driving a party of Canadian newspapermen, with me beside her.

Not once in our conversation did she realize I was a novice in England. I had learned by this time that a stove was a cooker, a truck a lorry, a sweater a jumper, a puff or comforter an eiderdown in England and a quilt in Scotland, an elevator a lift in England and an elevator again in Scotland.

I knew, of course, that gas was petrol, a car's hood a bonnet, a windshield a windscreen, a fender a mudguard, a trunk a boot. (At Newcastle on Tyne a public-relations man had come hurrying out of a factory handing me a carton of printed material and saying: "Here — put this in your boot!" I almost felt like handing him a pumpkin and saying, "Stick this up your shirtsleeve!" I hadn't been so surprised since my first yacht trip when the skipper called to me: "Stuart — grab the painter!" and I looked around frantically for a man in white coveralls to grab.)

When the lady chauffeur spoke of carriageways, I guessed immediately they were roads. Flyovers, I similarly grasped, were overpasses. "Slip roads" off cloverleafs (roundabouts) were exactly that. I could comprehend lay-bys. And motorways was an obvious synonym for expressways or thruways or parkways.

Only one term stuck me momentarily.

I noticed a big wooden box by the roadside, labelled "Grit".

"What is grit?" I asked innocently. Somehow I associated "grit" with what you feed chickens for their crop; it didn't occur to me that it meant sand.

"Grit?" she said absently. "Grit is — well, grit!"

"Oh," I said hopelessly. "I see."

"Right," she said brightly. "For when the road is icy."

It just shows that, with patience, anyone can understand the English.

Family Travel
Can Be Fun

Just by following a simple set of rules, any husband should be able this summer to enjoy an automobile trip with the wife and kids — able to handle any problem that arises.

Of course, only a few things ever go wrong on a family vacation, anyway. The trouble is that the same things keep going wrong all the time.

By mastering these little emergencies, then, the trip should become a pleasure!

1. *"I feel positive we've forgotten something."* This plaint from a worried wife — followed by "We always forget something, you know," and then, "Do you suppose we left the stove on?" — has a contagious effect. Soon the children are frantic. They can imagine the house going up in smoke with all its valuables — the electric train, the panda, and the false nose with moustache and spectacles attached.

The solution is easy. Put only one of your rubbers in the car when leaving on the trip. A few minutes later, when your wife wonders aloud, "Do you think we left the house windows open?" look down and exclaim, "Say — isn't that silly? I brought only one of my rubbers!" They will all laugh at you for being a fool, and your wife will say it's certainly a good thing your head is stuck on or you'd forget it too; but that doesn't matter. Now everyone knows what has been forgotten. The tension is broken.

2. *"That looks like a good place to eat — let's stop there!"* Never let your wife say this. It only upsets the children — because by the time you've taken in what she said, the restaurant is half a mile behind. The kids immediately get hungry, thinking of all the food back there they've missed forever. They begin to wail. Solution: Carry an emergency picnic lunch.

3. *"That looks like a nice picnic spot — let's stop there!"* The very same trouble. Naturally, when you realize she is talking to you, you're a mile past, wedged in the thick traffic stream. It does no good to assure her you'll watch out for the next picnic site because, as everyone knows, there is a curious phenomenon about picnic sites: The hungrier you get, the scarcer they become. The best ones are found in profusion immediately after the family has, in desperation, eaten on a dry spot of turf between a muskrat swamp and a piggery. Solution: Make a point of stopping at the very first picnic site, whether everyone is hungry or not. If you stop long enough, they will be.

4. *"Mummy, what is there to do?"* Youngsters get restless looking at the scenery going by. And no wonder: There's nothing to see except scenery. They yawn, argue over who's taking too much of the seat, put their heads out the window, lean their chins on the driver's shoulder, and, when told to sit back, stretch their feet under his seat and hoist him up.

For a tranquillizing remedy, suggest this happy game: Whoever sees each cow first gets one point; a horse, five points; a sheep, ten points; a cemetery, fifty points.

"It's a swell idea!" testifies my neighbor Fred Frolley. "We covered ninety-six miles in peace before the winner reached a hundred points. Of course, I was lucky — we went through quite a stretch of dense woods."

Herb Frobisher, who lives down the street, is equally enthusiastic. "When my kids got fed up merely earning points, I promised them cents. We got from Halifax to Rimouski for only $7.83!" Myself, I consider that a bit high. As long as he was going to hand out money, he might have changed the point system. I think he paid far too much for his cemeteries.

5. *"Mummy, I feel sick."* Some people treat the common car-sickness hazard by giving children pills. This is unnecessary. As I told Herb Frobisher, "Just feed them before you start — stuff 'em well — fill 'em up — and you'll have no problem." I don't think Herb gave it a fair try, though. He turned around after ten miles and said anxiously, "You kids sure you're O.K.? Nobody getting squalmish yet? None of

you starting to feel sick to your stomach, are you?" He seemed quite provoked at me for what happened almost immediately afterwards.

I gave Fred Frolley an even better anti-sickness tip, passed on to me by a man who owned a high-strung collie. "Let a chain drag behind your car. I don't know why, but it always works." It did, too. Fred told me every motorist coming up behind honked him to a stop and said, "You've got something loose." The kids got so interested they forgot to be sick.

6. *"Dear, I'm absolutely sure we're on the wrong road."* There's nothing like this remark from your wife to panic the kids. They think you're heading into a labyrinth for life.

Luckily, the remedy is very simple: Don't give her a road map to spread over her knees; say the gas station didn't have any. Give her a blanket instead. Every so often, stop the car, excuse yourself, go into the woods, take a road map out from under your shirt and examine it. This may be a nuisance, especially if you are a fellow who needs a map to get out of the woods again. But it's better than having the kids think you're about to drive the family over the edge of the world.

7. *"Where is there a bathroom?"* Children have an amazing knack for timing this. When you hear the question asked, you can be sure of two things: (a) in a moment they'll all take up the chorus; (b) there will be no place to stop for miles. For some reason they always say it when driving through heavily settled residential areas, never in the woods. Even when you think you are in the woods, it's only a delusion. If you stop, you'll see a house peeking out at you from behind those three trees. Children apparently have an inexplicable instinct for sensing when they are near homes (and bathrooms). Or it may be that home builders deliberately pick sites where they can catch motoring parties off guard.

Solution: Stop at every service station. Make sure all the kids get out. At least it will keep the gas tank full.

8. *"Mummy, my foot's asleep!"* This is a cinch. When you stop at a service station, march everybody up and down. This limbers them up and it gets quick service, too. Even the

manager comes running, thinking you're hunting frantically for a gas attendant and making his place look bad.

In Fred Frolley's case, I understand, they even gave him the gas for nothing to get him out fast. The manager said, "Everyone thinks the place is being picketed."

Herb Frobisher had an odd experience, too. After he'd marched his family up and down only twice, a man in white coveralls sidled out of the garage and whispered hoarsely to his wife, "Ladies to the left, gents to the right." She laughed appreciatively and kept marching; the man looked surprised. Until Herb explained it to her later, she thought the man was a card. She thought he was making a joke about square-dance calling.

9. *"Daddy, you look just like getting up on Sunday morning."* This should be sufficient warning of the most common fault that tourists lapse into — they start out on the trip looking neat and well-groomed, but after a few miles they get slovenly and slipshod. The driver doesn't know anyone any more; nobody knows him; he doesn't care. He lets his hair blow in his eyes. His shirt is unbuttoned. His bare stomach is sprinkled with cigarette ashes.

Stop, then, freshen up, and clean out the car before entering the next town, so you won't look like tourists. The worst possible thing, as every tourist knows, is to look like a tourist. If you arrive in a town and get out of the car looking dishevelled, beat up, creased, wrinkled, cramped and bent, and walk as stiffly as a lobster for the first half hour, you mark yourself an easy victim for the people who overcharge tourists. If you can contrive to make yourself look like a native, you are much better off. The prices won't be any lower, but you will get numerous extras — a parking ticket, probably, and even, with a little luck, a local jury summons.

10. *"Daddy, when are we going to find a place to sleep?"* This obsession sounds strange in kids who, back home, defiantly stay up all hours unless driven toward their bedrooms with a cat-o'-nine-tails. Their persistent query arises right after supper, aggravated by your wife's growing certainty that all the motels must be full by now. This is because people

are stopping earlier every year — even as early as 1 P.M. this season — to beat each other out.

I have hit on the idea of stopping at a motel at noon, and sleeping till 9 P.M., then driving through the night. You miss the scenery, but you sure cross up the mob.

These are my recommendations for dealing with the worst problems of family touring — the outcome of fifteen years of seeking a happy formula for happy holidays.

I was sure now, at last, I had all the answers. I was all set for a carefree vacation with the children.

Unfortunately, meanwhile, the kids had grown up.

... and Other Stories

How to Show Your Appreciation in a Zestful, Palate-Tingling Way

" . . . *again next week* at the same time. And now this is Kyle Pfeffersmidt reminding you that when you try the wonderful, sunny-brown, flavor-packed, baked-in goodness of Old Beanpot Vitaminized Beans, you'll say, 'Thank you, Kyle Pfeffersmidt, for tipping me off to this taste-tantalizing treat.' So get some from your grocer tomorrow — and don't forget to tell him Kyle Pfeffersmidt sent you! Tell him you rocked to old Kyle's Merry Music Moods tonight and you want to show your appreciation to Kyle Pfeffersmidt in a practical, zestful, palate-tingling way! So long, and keep Kyling!"

Do I ever enjoy that show! I went right into Beetwill's grocery store the next morning — I'd never been there before — and said as directed, "Kyle Pfeffersmidt sent me."

Mr. Beetwill looked puzzled. He said to the girl, "Do we have an order for any Pfeffersmidt?" She shook her head. He eyed me suspiciously, as if I were trying to get away with something.

"Oh, you don't understand," I smiled. "Kyle Pfeffersmidt is the orchestra leader; he's in a night club in New York."

Mr. Beetwill frowned, perplexed. "That's a thousand miles away. He probably gets his groceries in New York, too."

"I don't want his groceries," I said. "I just want a can of beans."

Mr. Beetwill looked at the girl and tapped the side of his head — apparently he wanted her to think harder.

"Certainly," he said, eyeing me strangely. "Any special brand?"

To my dismay, I couldn't remember. The name eluded me. "Oh, you know," I said. "Kyle Pfeffersmidt's beans."

Mr. Beetwill's face sagged. He whispered agitatedly to the girl. She vanished out back.

A moment later she reappeared carrying a carton on which was scrawled: "Mr. Fefrsmitt . . . To Call."

"Why, here you are!" Mr. Beetwill exclaimed. "How do you like that? We had your friend's order all the time — weren't we stupid? Now take it, please, and go quietly."

"Are you sure these are his beans?" I asked. The label on the can said Grandpap's Own Supergrade; it didn't sound right.

"Absolutely positive," Mr. Beetwill affirmed heartily, wrapping the can and thrusting it across the counter at me. "He phoned just a moment ago. Oh, don't bother to pay. I'll just charge it to Mr. Fef — to your friend's account. Good-bye now!"

Then I remembered what else Kyle Pfeffersmidt had asked me to say. I announced, "I rocked to old Kyle's Merry Music Moods last night."

Mr. Beetwill seemed taken aback momentarily. Then he cleared his throat — I could have sworn he winked at the girl — and said, "We had a nice evening too. We had Aunt Mabel over."

I added, "I'm here to show my appreciation in a practical, zestful, palate-tingling way."

Hastily Mr. Beetwill replied, "Don't do it here, please. Don't bother. That will be all right." He looked tense.

I walked out, carrying the parcel. Almost at once I heard the door slam behind me and the lock click.

A few steps down the street I looked back. They were both peering curiously from the display window.

I guess they don't sell a can of Grandpap's Own Supergrade beans very often.

Carry Me
Back to
Old Hypochondria

The authoritative health articles that are so popular today — the ones that tell you all about the newest ailments and what symptoms to watch out for — are bringing amazing benefits to my friends.

"How are you this lovely morning?" I asked Hector O'Dea on the street. He seemed bent over. I was surprised.

"Awful," he replied proudly. "I've got a contingency of the dithyramb."

"Gosh — sounds bad."

"Yes, isn't it!" He was beaming. He looked elated. "It's the very latest thing. I was lucky — just happened to read about it last night."

"Did you ever have it before?"

"How could I?" He appeared annoyed at my stupidity. "The doctors only discovered it last month."

He hobbled away cheerily.

A moment later Mrs. Brillson hobbled along.

"Good day," I said. "A lovely morning!"

"It *would* be," she admitted, "if I didn't have a touch of contingency of the dithyramb. It's simply dreadful."

But she looked as happy as a hummingbird. And no wonder. "I'm the very first in my bridge club to get it," she informed me. "It just came out this week."

I soon saw it was an epidemic. All my friends had it. They'd read Dr. Kotshz's health article about contingency of the dithyramb — by a remarkable coincidence, just as they were coming down with it. This was proved by the fact that in all cases the symptoms appeared within a matter of minutes afterward. They were all eager to tell me what terrible shape they were in. I was a good one to tell, because I didn't have it. I was shapeless. I hadn't read the article.

That's the wonderful thing I find about health articles

these days. The doctors who write them have a sixth sense. Their timeliness is astonishing. They know exactly what illnesses are going to strike my friends, and when.

Naturally my friends are pretty grateful — because if they didn't read the articles they'd never realize they had anything. They'd have to get better without even knowing they were sick.

Take Fred Frolley, now. The time he read Dr. Harolaya's treatise on the new affluvial pneumonia he couldn't get out of bed for two days. It nearly killed him. He made a quick recovery after reading the Rev. Norman Gordon Sopwith's article in the same issue, "You're Brimful Of Positive Vitality," but unfortunately turned the page and read Dr. O'Garrity's dissertation, "Common Symptoms Of Hyperbolic Tension," which snapped him back into bed again until the tension had run its course.

And Walter Holburn — he can hardly find words to say how thankful he is to Profs. Blattner and Deichs for writing their article, "Ambulant Phases Of Extremital Numbness." The very next morning he woke up with his right arm completely paralyzed.

His wife got so fussed up she called four doctors. They were pretty furious, standing around Walter's bed at 7 A.M., because by then his Extremital Numbness was all better. The doctors insist to this day he was only sleeping with his arm under his head, but Walter swears he was saved by the article, which enabled him to diagnose the affliction immediately and yell at his wife to call the doctor.

I could mention, too, Bill Bartley nearly choking to death before his wife got the Good Cheer Happy Health Column away from him — the one about precipitate paroxysms — and Herb Frobisher doubling up on the floor after only the third paragraph of Dr. Darwell's Helpful Hints, the day he announced the discovery of acute refraction of the esophagus. But these were comparatively slow-developing cases. They couldn't hold a candle to my attacks. By an ironic twist of fate I get definite symptoms even before I arrive at the third paragraph. I must be full of floating ailments just waiting to be recognized.

111

For instance a health article says:

"It has just been disclosed that medical science has identified a sinister creeping affliction known as barisytosilis."

The moment I start reading this, I'm done for. The size of the name sends a chill up my spine immediately, so I get my first symptom before I even know what it's all about.

"Barisytosilis," says the article, "will inevitably kill the victim within twelve days." That's the stuff I love to read — something good and fatal. I can hardly wait to learn the symptoms.

"The ailment first manifests itself," it continues, "in a decided pain in the right hip."

I no sooner read it than I feel it — quite a sharp pain, too. It seems to be just about where I'm sitting on the pocket comb with the broken teeth in my right hip pocket.

"This occurrence is accompanied by a pronounced drowsiness."

Come to think of it, my head *has* been getting heavy. In fact, I have all I can do now to keep it from lolling on my chest, though the clock on the mantel says it's not much past 1 A.M.

" . . . and severe aches in the arms."

This clinches it. It's uncanny. A moment ago, as I sat leaning on my elbows reading the article, I wasn't even conscious that I had arms. Now I'm suddenly aware both of them have been aching quietly for some time. Not acutely — but if I sit and listen for the pain I can feel it in the elbows, and the more I listen the worse it gets.

The morning after I read this I hurried to see Dr. McKetterich. Five minutes later he clicked the stethoscope together, stuffed it in his pocket and shook his head.

"You might as well put your shirt back on. I can't find a thing."

That's an odd quirk I've noticed about doctors. They're inventing new diseases all the time — they have more to choose from today than ever before — but they hate to let a patient have one of them. They want to hoard them all for themselves.

I waited the twelve days just to show Dr. McKetterich —

but I was still alive. This was a little disappointing, as he could gloat over me. But it wasn't really a surprise, because the fatal illnesses I read about never seem to kill me within the specified time. I think I must have inherited an exceptionally strong constitution.

Fortunately just then I picked up another article with more information about barisytosilis, and took new heart. It fitted me exactly, too!

Hurrying back with it to Dr. McKetterich's office, I knew better than to expect much satisfaction. I'd learned from experience that he resented my being cleverer than he was at his own game. I'd never been able to make him confess anything was wrong with me even when I showed him the article. But it was worth a try —

"Look at this!" I exclaimed. "It says here — 'Patients with barisytosilis are obsessed with an anxious fear that something terrible is going to happen to them.' I'm obsessed with an anxious fear that I'm going to get barisytosilis. So I must have barisytosilis already!"

He wouldn't admit it. He just sighed.

"I think," he said, "you'd better be running along."

Did you catch that? He's always wanting to get me out of his office quick like that, because he knows I show him up.

"As a matter of fact," I replied to put him in his place, "it so happens I've read six health articles in the last fortnight and seen two of those medical shows — 'Physic' — and it may surprise you to know I'm dead certain I have seven different diseases."

"It does surprise me," he said. "I'd expect you would have eight."

"I can explain that," I said helpfully. "One of the shows was about obstetrics."

He regarded me with a peculiar look as he rose slowly from his chair.

"If you don't get out, something terrible *is* going to happen to you."

He didn't clarify this. Doctors never say much. But I left happy, because it was the nearest I'd got to getting him to admit that I did have barisytosilis.

How to Sell
Tickets

Is it difficult to sell tickets to your friends for amateur concerts?

Do you start out with forty tickets to sell, and still have forty guiltily in your pocket when the chairman of the "progress luncheon" confidently calls for a report from each member?

Do you constantly marvel at where all the people in the concert audience come from? (Obviously *somebody* sells tickets to them; they would hardly be fool enough to buy them of their own free will.)

Then I can help you. I have discovered the secret of how the successful ticket sellers do it.

You will understand, of course, that our Merry Men's Glee Club concerts are not the usual run of amateur stuff. They are practically as good as professional; our director, Mr. Tiffle, has freely admitted this himself, and says the big audiences prove it.

But I never could sell a single ticket to my friends among the other department managers of the Consolidated Wrench and Belt Corporation. Goodness knows it wasn't for lack of trying. I would go right up to them and say, "You wouldn't like a ticket for the Merry Men's concert, would you?" and they readily agreed with me that they wouldn't.

So I began saying, "You do want tickets to the Merry Men's concert, don't you?" This didn't work either. Their faces showed a momentary twinge of pain, as if they had just remembered the rent for last month wasn't paid. It always seemed to be my luck to catch them at the wrong time, just when they were starting to think of something unpleasant.

In their pre-occupation with whatever was bothering them

114

they would say, "See me on Wednesday afternoon," completely forgetting Wednesday was their afternoon off.

So I asked Mr. Tiffle how he always sells sixty tickets. "I just distribute them among the staff at my store," he explained. "They each buy two."

"Don't they feel they have to?"

"Not at all," said Mr. Tiffle. "They realize if the boss thinks it's a good concert, it must be good."

It had never occurred to me that the brass polishers in my department might enjoy the Merry Men. I sent tickets to all of them, with a note carefully pointing out: "Do not think you must buy these. Refusal will not affect your job. A frank answer will be appreciated."

Everybody bought the tickets except one fellow who brought his back to me and said, "Frankly, I'd rather sit home and listen to Larrupin' Larry on TV."

Can you imagine the nerve, comparing a cultural group like the Merry Men with a cheap Ol' Opry star? As a matter of fact, I always did suspect the fellow of lacking judgment. Next Saturday I'm going to get rid of that misfit and put someone reliable in his job.

Two Cheese
Sandwiches

A news dispatch from a national dairy convention says: "The future of Canada's cheese industry depends to a great extent on whether you, as a Canadian, will eat the equivalent of two cheese sandwiches a week. Surely this is not too big a favor to ask."

Dear me, no; of course it isn't. I can't promise which day each week it will be, but I will certainly get those two sandwiches eaten if it will increase the home cheese market to 91,000,000 pounds a year, as the dispatch says, and then "the cheese industry will never have to worry very much about the outlook beyond our own borders."

I'm afraid, though, that I will have to worry about my own borders. They have been expanding steadily since the day I first realized that my eating habits, which were simply keeping me alive, were serving no useful purpose. Instead of selfishly eating to stay alive I should have been eating to keep the country prosperous whether I lived or not.

The truth came to me when I heard a fisheries marketing expert say on the car radio that his industry could be saved if I would eat three more pounds of fish every year. Surely, he added, this was not too big a favor to ask of a public-spirited citizen.

Immediately I arranged for my household to get public-spirited. It was easy. We just cut out bacon for breakfast and had fried smelt instead. But then a hog marketing expert called over the radio that if I would just eat four extra pounds of bacon every year Canada wouldn't have to worry about the loss of British orders. So we put the bacon back on the menu, and of course we left the fish there too, because it was no good to be half public-spirited.

As the months went by, and word got around among the

other marketing experts that I was cleaning up the fish and bacon surpluses and might as well be working on theirs too in my spare time, the urgent appeals came thick and fast for me to eat more and oftener. I added an extra dish of oatmeal at breakfast to help out the Western farmers, an extra glass of milk so the cows wouldn't burst, and an extra fried egg to stabilize the Rhode Island Reds. (In case you are wondering, as I did, whether they should be put through a loyalty check first, they are not Communists. They are a baseball team.)

We were puzzled at first about how to use up the extra butter we agreed to eat, until it struck me we should be eating an extra potato or two every meal to help out the New Brunswick growers, who have shown enough initiative to raise too many potatoes but not enough to hire propagandists to urge me to eat them up. Nothing goes better with potatoes than butter, and vice versa.

I don't know just where on my schedule I'll be able to work in those two cheese sandwiches, unless perhaps around 11 o'clock on Wednesday morning, when, I see, I have a free hour after eating two apples to save Nova Scotia orchardists.

It would be appreciated if the marketing experts, as a reciprocal gesture to save me, would suggest something sometime that I can drop out of my menu. At least they could walk down the hall in Ottawa and ask those fellows in the federal health department to stop urging me to follow a sensible moderate diet for the sake of the nation's physical fitness.

How the
Lawn-Chair Business
Folded Up

BESTWICK HOBBY BUILDERS LTD.
LONDON, ONT.

Mr. Milbert Jones,
Saint John, N.B.

Dear Mr. Jones:

We acknowledge with thanks your order for our Instruction Course, "Paddle Your Own Distinctive Home-Made Canoe" ($12.50). Your intention to embark on this advanced project is most interesting, as our files show only three months ago you purchased "Sit In Your Own Distinctive Home-Made Lawnchair" ($4.75), evidently with excellent success.

Would you be kind enough to write a Testimonial for our Catalogue, with a photo of yourself in the Lawnchair?

Yours with keen anticipation,
Henry P. Bestwick,
PRESIDENT

Mr. Henry P. Bestwick,
President, Bestwick Hobby Builders Ltd.,
London, Ont.

Dear Mr. Bestwick:

Enclosed please find photo, which is so distinctive it may surprise you. My Testimonial follows:

I went into lawnchairs with my neighbor Jim Hackleby. "The modern way is the assembly line," Jim said enthusiastically. "I'll make the arms and legs; you make the seats and slats. We'll put them together efficiently in one evening."

It was great fun. We kept phoning each other to see how we were doing.

118

"Hello!" Jim would say. "Arms and Legs Department speaking. Inter-Departmental Memo: How about a little game at the club tonight?"

I would say, "Seats and Slats. Request confirmed. Roger!"

Jim, of course, is a great kidder. Once he said, disguising his voice (I think by holding his nose): "Mammoth Furniture Stores speaking. Ship us 1,000 lawnchairs immediately." This made us feel pretty proud to think what an industry we had created.

Unfortunately, after we sawed enough pieces for a whole lawnchair, we never could seem to get together for the assembly job. One of us was always out. This provoked whoever was in.

When I finally heard my phone ring, I answered hopefully, "Seats and Slats," and a deep voice said, "Greetings this lovely evening, Mr. Jones. This is your new minister, Dr. Howland."

Irritably I replied, "Now see here, Arms and Legs. Stop talking like an idiot."

"I *beg* your pardon." Jim never sounded that deep.

In confusion I could only gasp, "Oh, Dr. Howland, you understand, I wasn't myself just then. I was Seats and Slats, and I thought you were Arms and Legs. See? We're an assembly line."

"That makes it entirely clear."

"Yes," I continued eagerly. "You see, I hoped to have everything put together long before this."

"Well, try and pull yourself together before Sunday. I expect to see you then."

On Sunday, I understand, he gave a temperance sermon on "Picking Up The Pieces." It may have been just a coincidence. In any case I felt quite angry at Jim.

Jim, I hear, kept answering every call expectantly, "Arms and Legs speaking," until his boss phoned about the mislaid Montreal account and suggested he try to find his head too. Jim felt I had played an underhand trick on him.

I don't know what he is doing with his arms and legs, but I discovered my seat fits admirably in a canoe. So I hope to interest another neighbor, Percy Truskett, in making canoes from your book and I will make the seats and back slats, which I am very good at.

Yours appreciatively,
Milbert Jones

P. S.: The snapshot of me sitting in one of my lawn-chairs on the lawn doesn't show my slats, as there was no way to hold them together for the picture, due to the lack of arms and legs. It doesn't show my seat, either, as I am sitting on it. However, people say it is a fine likeness.

120

You're Darn Tootin'

The wonderful idea came to me by sheer chance.

I drove up beside a car full of people in the next traffic lane waiting for the light. Their rear turn-signal had been flashing for blocks.

I tooted. The driver looked over. Through the closed window I waved, flipping my thumb downward toward the rear of his car.

Smiling, he nodded to me, wondering where he had met me or whom I'd mistaken him for.

I waved again, pointing my thumb conspicuously downward.

He seemed surprised at my friendliness.

Still smiling, he waved back, pointing his thumb the same way. He thought it was a lodge greeting.

I kept waving, more vigorously. He stared back; he was beginning to look uneasy now.

"Your *turn-signal*!" He couldn't hear me with our windows closed and the engines idling. So I pointed down with my forefinger.

He looked down around his feet. All the women in the back seat looked down, too, to see if their stockings were laddered.

I shook my head agitatedly.

He opened his door, hauled himself half out, peered at his tires. Then he frowned at me suspiciously. His look meant: "Whaddya mean, scaring a guy like that?" He slammed his door.

In despair I toot-toot-tooted. I pointed repeatedly toward the back of his car, my forefinger going like a woodpecker's head.

Suddenly he gave a sign of understanding. He swivelled

around and looked through his rear window. He nodded to me gratefully. He got it now: The man behind was drunk!

His traffic line started to move. My friend was too smart. He didn't budge. He put his arm out, waving the driver to pass. He wasn't going to take chances on any lunkhead smacking into his trunk at the next light.

After a moment, the car crept around him. The man at the wheel wagged his head at him sympathetically: Poor chap, to have his engine conk out in traffic! The new motorist had his collar on backward. He was a clergyman.

As my own line started, I caught a glimpse of my friend. His face was working; he seemed apoplectic. Our windows being shut, I couldn't hear what he was saying, but he was saying something; his face looked like a TV baritone singing with the sound turned off.

Which was how it happened, the very next day at the Little Moose Club, I originated honky-talk.

"In all these years," I told the boys, "motorists have never learned to communicate properly with each other — they can't talk by blowing their own horns. What this world needs is a Language of Cars!"

The idea made an instant hit.

A simple code system for automobile horns, everyone agreed, would be a boon to millions of drivers — the most important international language yet.

As Herb Frobisher aptly put it — Herb's always quick to see things — "I've heard of the Language of Love, the Language of Diplomacy and the Language of Flowers. But what good are *they*?"

We all readily concurred. None of us knew many lovers, but those we knew didn't seem to talk much. We knew fewer diplomats; but it was common knowledge in the Little Moose Club they had got the world into an awful mess — in fact, our own members could have done as well; they often said so. As for the Language of Flowers, nobody knew anyone who talked to flowers.

It took no time to figure out that by using combinations of only four toots — short or long, like Morse — we could invent twenty-six different messages!

122

"You've got a flat," "You're taking the wrong turn," "You can go ahead," "Stop, I want to speak with you," "How many miles to the nearest restroom?" "There's a policeman behind you" — it was amazing how fast we found ourselves thinking up signals to send.

Everybody was excited over the possibilities.

"Just imagine, for instance," exclaimed Bill Bartley, "what a help the Language of Cars could be to motorists caught in a traffic jam!"

We all agreed the present language between cars caught in a traffic jam was terrible.

When the time came to memorize the twenty-six messages, however, quite a few of the boys didn't show up. I'm sure it wasn't that they lost interest — it's just that members of today's community clubs are given so many trifling things to do they completely forget the really important things.

But the four of us who did show up were enthusiastic.

We tried out the system right away in the card room.

I shuffled along making a noise like a car engine.

"Toot-toot . . . toot . . . tooooot!" said Sam McCool right behind me.

I turned around quickly: "My trunk lid was flapping open?"

"Cor-*rect*!" delightedly. "Right on the button!"

See the usefulness of it? If my trunk lid had only been flapping open, I'd have known.

We could hardly wait to test our honky-talk on car drivers. We knew they'd get to learn it gradually, just by hearing it.

Herb Frobisher was about to park his new car downtown the next afternoon when, happily, he noticed a car ahead with its muffler dragging.

"Toooooooooot!" he signalled. "Toooooooooot!" (pause) "Toooooooooot!" (pause) "Toooooooooot!" This was the prolonged danger warning for a damaged car.

The driver didn't even look around. Of course, motorists didn't know the language yet.

"Toooooooooot!" (pause) "Toooooooooot!"

No response.

"Toooooooooot!" (pause) "Toooooooooot!"

From somewhere above, possibly on the fourth or fifth floor, Herb heard a man's voice bawl, "Somebody stop that blasted kid!"

"Toooooooooot!" (pause) "Toooooooooot!"

Suddenly — *crash* — an explosion rocked Herb. He thought some fool had bumped him. He saw broken glass on the street, the remains of an ink bottle. He got out and looked. His roof was dented!

I don't know why it should, but Herb's enthusiasm for our project seemed to wane from that very day. At least he never came back to the club.

Bill Bartley, the same week, stopping for a traffic light at an intersection, was thrilled to see a car beside him with a door ajar. This was easy: Signal No. 4.

"Toot-de-toooot-toooot!"

The other driver paid no attention.

"Toot-de-toooot-toooot!"

Still no reaction.

Bill, I'm glad to say, isn't easily discouraged. He kept it up, knowing it was sure to get results eventually. It did.

A traffic cop strolled over, writing a ticket! Can you imagine, calling one of *us* a public nuisance? It cost Bill $2 on the spot, but not before a uniformed girl carhop ran out from Frank's Hamburger Bar and handed Bill, to his surprise, a cardboard plate with a hot hamburger, French fries and coffee. This cost him 95 cents.

Bill hasn't been back to the club yet, either.

But Sam McCool, fortunately, was made of stauncher stuff. He stuck with the ship. Twitting didn't faze him a bit. (There are always envious people who ridicule the pioneers in any new movement.) Sam just laughed it off when a wit asked him on the street if he was going out on a toot tonight. When he got a letter addressed to Little Bo Beep-Beep, he didn't even open it.

You have to admire a fellow like Sam. He didn't quit even when it became apparent the whole town was turning against us because we were pioneers. It certainly wasn't our fault if the teenage crowd took up honky-talk too, though many people seemed to think it was Sam or myself every

124

time they heard a jalopy horn making like a wolf call. The place just became hyper-sensitive about cars tooting. Whenever a young moron roared through the streets at 2 A.M. blatting his horn, Sam or I got roused out of bed by another indignant phone call saying we ought to be ashamed of ourselves.

Sam was merely driving over to my house early one evening, to suggest that perhaps we should give the whole idea a rest until the public was more ready for it, when one of those things happened that can happen to any motorist.

As he stopped for a traffic light at a busy corner, his new horn short-circuited — the horn with the loud high-pitched note he'd bought especially for honky-talking. It wouldn't stop blowing.

"Toooooooooooooooooooooooooooooooooooooooooo——!"

Before Sam, completely rattled, could collect his senses:

1. A crowd gathered on the sidewalk.

2. Two girls came out of their houses, primping their hair, looking up and down the street for their boy friends.

3. An automobile mechanic hurried over, recognized Sam, realized it couldn't be a horn stuck, and walked away.

4. Night-shift workers on their way to the fish-paste factory began to sprint, thinking their watches were wrong.

5. The driver of the truck ahead stomped back and tried to punch Sam through the open window.

6. His wife flew at him from the other side.

7. Nervous old Mrs. Birtle, ready-packed suitcase in hand, came flying down her front steps heading for the basement, thinking the nuclear missile war had started.

8. The same policeman sauntered over and thrust a ticket through Sam's window.

9. When the policeman hollered in his ear to stop it, and Sam hollered back unintelligibly he couldn't, he got a summons for wilfully obstructing the law and sassing a peace officer.

10. Sam jumped out and fled.

As he ran, he could hear his car calling after him plaintively —

"ooooooooooooooooooooooooooooooooooooooooo——!"

So you can see, it's all been worth while. Although I'm the only member of our movement left, I'm pretty happy to think how honky-talk-conscious our town has become at last. I'd congratulate Sam for proving that people *can* be made to pay attention, if I could only find him.

How I Missed
the Flu

People are still talking about their experiences in last winter's flu epidemic and are looking forward eagerly to the next one. I feel left out of every conversation, because I have nothing to talk about. I didn't get the flu.

When it hit our office, Mrs. McCormick, the cashier, told me, "If you're wise you'll do what my family did in 1918. Put some bear grease up your nose and sip a few teaspoons of Irish whiskey morning and night and let it roll around your tongue. It's wonderful protection."

"Then you didn't get the flu in 1918?"

"Well, yes, I did, toward the end of it. But I didn't mind it so much. It wasn't bad at all."

I didn't take this treatment, because when I went to ask Mrs. McCormick the next day whether Scotch whiskey would do as well, and where to get a bear and how I could tell a greasy one from the others, she was gone. She was home with the flu, and having, I imagine, a hilarious time with it. She didn't come back for three weeks, and I don't blame her.

Miss Gladwyn, who was hired temporarily to fill her place, told me I should get some of the large white tablets she was taking three times a day. "They're a prescription of old Dr. Thompson's," she said. "He gave it to me only a month before he died. I don't know what they are but they're the only thing in the world that does any good. Do you know whose word I have for that?"

I said I couldn't offer a guess; I presumed it was Sir William Osler.

"Billy Doherty, the druggist, told me so himself. He said very few people have found out about the tablets."

She paused to let the effect sink in, and I looked properly impressed. Naturally the druggists, who make up the prescriptions, are in the best possible position to know which medicines the doctors prescribe only rarely, so as not to give away trade secrets or let people get better too fast.

Miss Gladwyn promised to bring the prescription next morning. Unfortunately she didn't come back; she took the flu, and before she got better Mrs. McCormick had returned to work, a little wobbly on her legs and smelling rancid but in high good spirits.

So, unable to take advantage of anybody's treatment in time, I missed the flu completely. I was forced to go through the entire epidemic season without even a sniffle to talk about.